NEW YORK ARCHITECTURE

NEW YORK ARCHITEKTUR

NEW YORK ARCHITECTUUR

ARQUITECTURA DE NUEVA YORK

NEW YORK ARCHITECTURE
NEW YORK ARCHITEKTUR
NEW YORK ARCHITECTUUR
ARQUITECTURA DE NUEVA YORK

Julio Fajardo
Mariana Eguaras Etchetto

FKG

F K G

Editorial project:
2010 © **LOFT Publications**
Via Laietana, 32, 4.º, Of. 92
08003 Barcelona, Spain
Tel.: +34 932 688 088
Fax: +34 932 687 073
loft@loftpublications.com
www.loftpublications.com

Created and distributed in cooperation
with Frechmann Kolón GmbH
www.frechmann.com

Editorial coordinator:
Simone K. Schleifer

Assistant to editorial coordination:
Aitana Lleonart

Editor:
Julio Fajardo
Mariana Eguaras Etchetto

Art director:
Mireia Casanovas Soley

Design and layout coordination:
Claudia Martínez Alonso

Cover layout:
Ignasi Gracia Blanco

Layout:
Cristina Simó Perales

Translations:
Equipo de Edición (English, German, French, Italian)
Cillero & de Motta (Dutch)

ISBN:
978-84-92731-86-2 (GB)
978-84-9936-120-8 (E)
978-80-556-0018-5 (SLOVART)

Printed in China

The Big Apple, cosmopolitan city par excellence, capital of the world; these are some of the adjectives that have defined New York over the course of history, although words are never quite enough to describe this fascinating and vibrating city. Its strategic geographical position, its historical record as the primary doorway open to the New World, its rapid economic growth and its role as a meeting point and gathering place for the cultures of the world make it a city that never stops re-inventing itself. New York's recent architecture illustrates this dynamic character. What several decades was possibly perceived as an obsessive appeal for skyscrapers and the creation of a singular skyline has now given way to a body of architecture that exhibits articulate forms, incorporates advanced construction systems, explores new materials and above all, seeks a continuous interaction with the city's inhabitants. The following pages propose a tour of the most recent corporate buildings, commercial spaces, museums, hotels, restaurants, bars and public spaces within the city. What perhaps in theory cannot be explained with words can be transmitted through the succession of images that comprise this edition, a complete and thorough study of the most recently constructed works and future projects of a city that continues to stand as a reference point for the contemporary architecture stage.

Big Apple, Hauptstadt der Welt, das sind einige der Bezeichnungen, mit denen man New York im Laufe seiner Geschichte zu definieren suchte. Jedoch kann man diese faszinierende und vibrierende Stadt nur schlecht mit Worten beschreiben. Da die Stadt eine sehr günstige, geographische Lage einnimmt und das Haupteingangstor zum neuen Kontinent war, ihre Wirtschaft mit Schwindel erregender Geschwindigkeit wächst und sie Treffpunkt für die Kulturen der Welt ist, definiert sie sich auch fortwährend selbst neu. Die neueste Architektur New Yorks ist ein Beweis für diese Dynamik. Was vor einigen Jahrzehnten noch als eine Leidenschaft für Wolkenkratzer und die Definition eines originellen städtischen Profils übersetzt wurde, ist nun zu einer Architektur geworden, die ansprechende Formen sucht, fortschrittliche Bausysteme benutzt, mit neuen Materialien experimentiert und vor allem eine interaktive Beziehung zu den Bewohnern aufbauen will. Auf den folgenden Seiten möchten wir Ihnen die neusten Firmengebäude und Einkaufszentren, Museen, Hotels, Restaurants, Kneipen, Cafés und öffentliche Einrichtungen der Stadt vorstellen. Das, was man vielleicht nicht so einfach mit Worten erklären kann, kann man an den Bildern dieses Bandes erkennen. Diese Zusammenstellung der neusten Bauten und künftigen Projekte der Stadt beweist, dass New York auch weiterhin ausschlaggebend für das Panorama der zeitgenössischen Architektur ist.

Grosse pomme, ville cosmopolite par excellence, capitale du monde, sont parmi les qualificatifs qui ont défini New York au cours de son histoire, même s'il n'existe pas assez de mots servant à décrire cette cité fascinante et vibrante. Sa position géographique stratégique, avoir été la principale porte d'entrée du nouveau continent, sa croissance économique vertigineuse et représenter le point de rencontre mondial des cultures permettent à cette ville de sans cesse se redéfinir. L'architecture récente de New York nous démontre ce dynamisme. Ce qui jusqu'à il y a quelques décennies se traduisait par une obsession pour les gratte-ciels et la définition d'un profil urbain original a laissé le pas à une recherche architectonique qui propose des volumes suggestifs, intègre des systèmes avancés de construction, innove dans des nouveaux matériaux et surtout tente d'obtenir une relation plus interactive avec ses habitants. Les pages suivantes nous proposent un parcours parmi les plus récents édifices corporatifs, espaces commerciaux, musées, hôtels, restaurants, bars et espaces publics de la ville. Ce qui au début n'est peut-être pas possible d'expliquer par des mots, peut être suggérer grâce aux images qui illustrent cette édition. Voici donc un reportage complet des dernières œuvres architecturales construites et des futurs projets d'une ville qui reste toujours la référence dans le panorama de l'architecture contemporaine.

Wie innoveert in New York, innoveert in de hele wereld. Ongeacht de discipline waarover men het heeft, zou het niet wijs zijn deze bewering te betwisten. De architectuur is in dit geval al helemaal geen uitzondering, niet alleen omdat de meest prestigieuze architecten -diegenen die trends zetten en de avant-garde definiëren- in de Big Apple hun hoofdkantoren hebben, maar ook omdat de begeerde percelen op het Eiland van Manhattan en omstreken ook het kader vormen van talrijke van de bijzonderste projecten van de meest erkende ontwerpers van de planeet. Vier jaar na het eerste, analyseert en actualiseert dit tweede volume van New York Architecture & Design de reeks voorbeelden die toen reeds veel succes boekten. Deze catalogus biedt opnieuw een gevarieerd repertorium van de beste architectuur die opgetrokken en gepland werd voor de stad van de wolkenkrabbers, zowel op residentieel, institutioneel als commercieel gebied. Een overzicht van de projecten die dit boek vormen zal een duidelijke visie geven van het dynamisme, de heterogeniteit, de stijl en de moderniteit dat de architectuur aan de visueel indrukwekkendste stad ter wereld verlenen. Deze pagina's vatten een zo gevarieerd mogelijk repertorium samen dat, naast de ligging van de projecten, slechts twee punten gemeen heeft: innovatie en uitmuntendheid.

Grande Mela, cittá cosmopolita per eccellenza, capitale del mondo, sono alcuni degli aggettivi che hanno definito nel tempo New York, anche se sempre sono poche le parole per descrivere quest'affascinante e vibrante cittá. La sua strategica posizione geografica, l'essere stata la principale porta d'entrata al nuovo continente, la sua vertiginosa crescita economica e l'essere il principale punto d'incontro mondiale delle culture, fa sí che questa cittá non finisca mai di definire se stessa. L'architettura piú recente di New York ci dimostra questo dinamismo. Quella che fino a poche decine di anni fa si poteva tradurre come un'ossessione per i grattacieli e per la creazione di un profilo urbano originale, ha lasciato il passo alla ricerca di un'architettura che propone volumi suggestivi, incorpora sistemi avanzati di costruzione, indaga nuovi materiali e soprattutto scopre una relazione piú interattiva coi suoi abitanti. Nelle pagine seguenti viene proposto un percorso attraverso i piú recenti edifici corporativi, spazi commerciali, musei, hotel, ristoranti, bar e spazi pubblici della cittá. Ció che forse é impossibile spiegare a parole si puó intravvedere attraverso le immagini che compongono questa pubblicazione, un reportage completo delle ultime opere costruite e dei progetti futuri di una cittá che continua ad essere un riferimento nel panorama dell'architettura contemporanea.

La Gran Manzana, ciudad cosmopolita por excelencia, capital del mundo: éstos son algunos de los adjetivos que han definido a Nueva York a lo largo de su historia, aunque siempre son pocas las palabras para describir a esta ciudad fascinante y vibrante. Su estratégica posición geográfica, su condición de principal puerta de entrada al nuevo continente, su vertiginoso crecimiento económico y su papel como punto de encuentro de culturas de todo el mundo hacen de Nueva York una ciudad que nunca cesa de reinventarse. Su arquitectura reciente ilustra este carácter dinámico. Lo que hasta hace algunas décadas se veía como una obsesión por los rascacielos y por la creación de un *skyline* urbano original ha dado paso a la búsqueda de una arquitectura que propone volúmenes sugerentes, incorpora avanzados sistemas de construcción, explora nuevos materiales y, sobre todo, busca una interacción con sus habitantes. En las siguientes páginas se propone un recorrido por los edificios corporativos, espacios comerciales, museos, hoteles, restaurantes, bares y espacios públicos más recientes de la ciudad. Lo que no sea posible explicar con palabras quizás se pueda comprender a través de las imágenes que componen esta edición, que recoge un completo reportaje de las últimas construcciones y de los proyectos futuros de una ciudad que sigue siendo un referente en el panorama de la arquitectura contemporánea.

Catherine Malandrino Boutique

The evocation of a European street marks the interior design of this boutique, whose space was conceived as a type of vantage point inspired by the Maeght terrace in Saint-Paul de Vence, France. An enormous Murano glass chandelier flows like a waterfall and crowns the establishment. Beneath it is the curved parquet flooring that delimits the route around the store. The showcase design wraps around and adapts to the style of the items on display, the French designer's elegant clothing and accessories collection.

La décoration de cette boutique évoque une rue européenne. L'espace a été conçu comme une sorte de mirador, inspiré de la terrasse Maeght de Saint-Paul de Vence. Un énorme lustre en verre de Murano tombe en cascade et couronne l'établissement. En dessous, le revêtement de sol aux lignes sinueuses dessine le parcours à l'intérieur de la boutique. La vitrine enveloppe et s'adapte au style des articles qui y sont exposés, l'élégante collection de vêtements et d'accessoires de la créatrice française.

L'evocazione di una via europea è l'elemento che definisce il design d'interni di questa *boutique*, il cui spazio è stato concepito come una specie di belvedere, ispirato alla terrazza Maeght di Saint-Paul de Vence. Un'enorme lampada ragno di cristallo di Murano cade come una cascata e corona lo stabilimento. Sotto di essa si spiega il parquet dalle forme curve che definisce il percorso del negozio. Il design dello *showcase* avvolge gli articoli esposti, l'elegante collezione di capi d'abbigliamento e accessori della stilista francese, e si adatta al loro stile.

Die Innengestaltung dieser Boutique hat die Anmutung einer Straße, wie man sie etwa in Europa finden kann. Die Raumkonzeption wurde durch die Terrasse der Maeght-Stiftung in Saint-Paul de Vence angeregt. Ein riesiger Kronleuchter aus Murano-Glas wirkt wie ein Wasserfall und krönt diese Geschäftsniederlassung. Darunter entfaltet sich der Parkettboden, der, in Kurven angelegt, den Weg durch das Geschäft markiert. Die Schaufläche umfasst die ausgestellten Artikel – die elegante Kleider- und Accessoirekollektion der französischen Modedesignerin – und ihre Gestaltung ist an deren Stil angepasst.

Het interieurontwerp van deze boetiek doet denken aan een Europese straat, waar de ruimte opgevat werd als een soort uitkijkplaats, geïnspireerd op het Maeght-terras in Saint-Paul de Vence, Frankrijk. Een enorme kroonluchter in Murano glas duikt op als een waterval en bekroont het etablissement. Daaronder ligt de bochtige parketvloer die de route doorheen de winkel aangeeft. De kledingrekken vertonen een ontwerp dat doorheen de ruimte slingert en zich aan de elegante kleding- en accessoirecollectie van de Franse ontwerpster aanpast.

La evocación de una calle europea marca el diseño de esta *boutique*, cuyo espacio fue concebido como una especie de mirador, inspirado en la terraza Maeght de Saint-Paul de Vence. Una enorme lámpara de araña de cristal de Murano cae como una catarata y corona el establecimiento. Bajo ella se despliega el entarimado de formas curvas que marca el recorrido de la tienda. El diseño del *showcase* envuelve y se adapta al estilo de los artículos que se exhiben, la elegante colección de ropa y los accesorios de la diseñadora francesa.

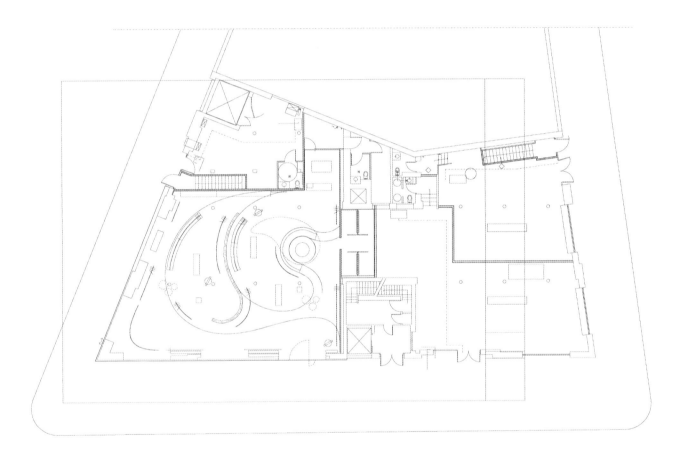

ALDEN MADDRY ARCHITECT

Phillipps-Skaife Residence

The chief challenge in this remodeling project was gaining space to provide light to the residence. For this purpose, glass panels were laid in the floor of the upper level, next to the stairs, to allow light to pass, and walls were removed. The same purpose was behind the use of translucent panels to separate the different spaces in the apartment's lower level.

Le défi principal à relever consistait à gagner de l'espace pour augmenter la luminosité du logement. Pour ce faire, des panneaux en verre ont été installés à l'étage, à côté de l'escalier, et des cloisons ont été abattues, permettant ainsi le passage de la lumière. Toujours dans la même optique, des panneaux translucides ont été utilisés comme séparateurs d'ambiance au rez-de-chaussée de l'appartement.

La principale sfida di questo intervento di ristrutturazione era dare maggiore spazio alla luminosità. A tal fine sono stati sistemati al piano alto dell'appartamento, accanto alla scala, dei pannelli di vetro per consentire il passaggio della luce e sono stati eliminati i tramezzi. Con lo stesso obiettivo, sono stati utilizzati dei pannelli traslucidi per separare gli ambienti al piano basso dell'appartamento.

Bei dieser Reform lag die Hauptherausforderung darin, Platz für den Lichteinfall in der Wohnung zu gewinnen. Zu diesem Zweck wurden im oberen Stock Glaspaneele neben die Treppe gebaut, um den Lichteinfall zu ermöglichen. Außerdem wurden Wände entfernt. Mit der gleichen Absicht wurden durchscheinende Paneele als Abtrennung der Ambientes im unteren Teil der Wohnung eingesetzt.

De belangrijkste uitdaging van deze verbouwing bestond erin ruimte te winnen voor een betere lichtinval. Daarvoor bracht men in de flat op de bovenverdieping, naast de trap, glazen panelen aan om het licht door te laten en werden er tussenwanden weggenomen. Met hetzelfde doel voor ogen werd gebruik gemaakt van doorschijnende panelen als scheidingswand tussen de vertrekken op de benedenverdieping.

El desafío principal de la reforma de esta vivienda consistió en ganar espacio para aumentar la luminosidad. Para ello, se colocaron en el piso de la planta alta, al lado de la escalera, unos paneles de vidrio para permitir el paso de la luz y se eliminaron los tabiques. Con el mismo fin, se utilizaron paneles traslúcidos a modo de separador de ambientes en la planta baja del piso.

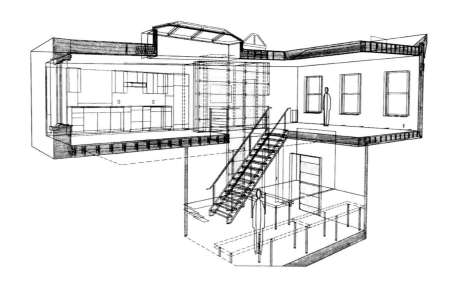

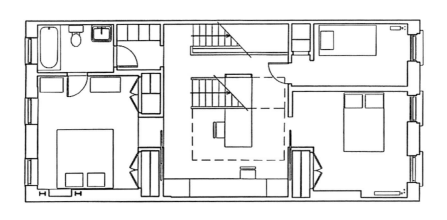

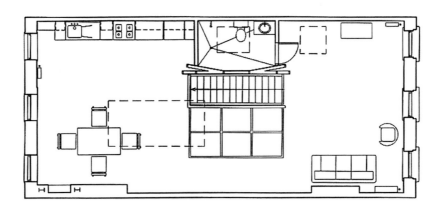

ALI TAYAR

Pizza Bar

The ultra-urban design of this pizzeria had to include a counter for the home-delivery service, a large dining area and a lounge zone. The spatial limitations of the floor were taken into account to ensure it did not look too crowded – a challenge it more than rose to. The 70s pop inspiration is undeniable. An exposed brick wall houses the booths with the tables in the dining area while the drinking area is delimited by a wooden floor at the back of the restaurant.

Cette pizzeria furieusement urbaine devait se composer d'un comptoir pour le service à domicile, d'une salle de restaurant spacieuse et d'un espace lounge. Il a fallu tenir compte des limitations spatiales des locaux pour que l'établissement ne paraisse pas encombré, et le résultat dépasse les objectifs de départ. Le style indubitablement pop s'inspire clairement des années 1970. Un mur de briques apparentes accueille les consoles avec les tables dans la salle de restaurant, et l'espace bar est délimité par le parquet au fond du restaurant.

Il design tremendamente urbano di questa pizzeria doveva includere un banco per il servizio a domicilio, un'ampia sala da pranzo e una zona lounge. Si è tenuto conto dei limiti spaziali affinché lo stabilimento non sembrasse troppo pieno, e il risultato è stato ampiamente conseguito. Lo stile pop chiaramente ispirato agli anni 70 è fuori discussione. Un muro di mattoni a vista ospita le console con i tavoli nella sala da pranzo, mentre la zona bar è circoscritta a una pedana in fondo al restaurante.

Das durch und durch urbane Design dieser Pizzeria musste eine Theke für die Abwicklung des Heimservice, außerdem ein geräumiges Restaurant und einen Lounge-Bereich integrieren. Die räumlichen Vorgaben des Grundrisses wurden berücksichtigt, indem der Raum luftig gestaltet wurde. Dass sich der Entwurf an den Popstil der Siebziger Jahre anlehnt, ist unumstritten. Im Restaurant sind Konsolen für die Tische in eine Mauer aus Sichtziegeln eingelassen; hingegen ist der Bereich, in dem nur Getränke zu sich genommen werden, auf ein Podium im hinteren Teil des Restaurants beschränkt.

De uitgesproken stadslook van deze pizzeria moet een toog omvatten voor de thuisbezorging, een ruime eetzaal en een loungeruimte. Er werd rekening gehouden met de ruimtelijke beperkingen om te vermijden dat het restaurant zou lijken, een doelstelling die ruimschoots bereikt werd. Er heerst onbetwistbare popartsfeer, geïnspireerd op de jaren zeventig. Een blote bakstenen muur begrenst de zitplaatsen met de eettafels in de eetzaal, terwijl de bar afgebakend wordt door een planken vloer achterin het restaurant.

El diseño rabiosamente urbano de esta pizzería debía incluir un mostrador para el servicio a domicilio, un amplio comedor y una zona *lounge*. Las limitaciones espaciales de la planta fueron tenidas en cuenta para que el establecimiento no pareciera abarrotado, lo cual se logró con creces. El estilo pop inspirado claramente en los 70 resulta incuestionable. Un muro de ladrillo visto alberga las consolas con las mesas en el comedor, mientras que la zona de copas se circunscribe a una tarima en el fondo del restaurante.

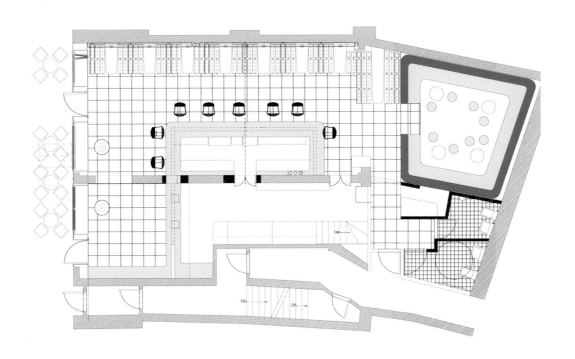

ALI TAYAR

Pop Burger

The design of this hamburger restaurant plays with three aspects of quintessential American cuisine: the fast-food joint, the Western saloon and the speakeasy. It combines two well-differentiated ambiances, i.e., the home-delivery service and fast food area which boasts an aluminum mural by Ronnie Cutrone, a former collaborator of Andy Warhol, and the bar, located at the back and featuring sheets of steel, oak and blue-tinted glass.

Ce restaurant de fast-food conjugue trois aspects qui représentent la quintessence de la gastronomie américaine : la restauration rapide, le salon Far West et le *speakeasy*. L'établissement combine deux atmosphères bien différenciées. D'un côté, le service à domicile et de restauration rapide, doté d'une œuvre murale en aluminium de Ronnie Cutrone, un ancien collaborateur d'Andy Warhol. Dans le bar aménagé au fond des locaux prédominent les plaques d'acier, le chêne et le verre teinté bleu.

Il design di questa paninoteca lega tra loro tre aspetti che esprimono la quintessenza gastronomica americana: il ristorante fast food, il saloon in stile western e lo *speakeasy*. Lo stabilimento combina due ambienti ben differenziati. Da una parte, il servizio a domicilio e di fast food, che possiede un murale di alluminio di Ronnie Cutrone, ex collaboratore di Andy Warhol. Con un ambiente molto distinto, nel bar allestito sul fondo predominano le piastre d'acciaio, il legno di quercia e il vetro colorato in toni blu.

Die Gestaltung dieses Hamburger-Restaurants vereinigt drei Aspekte, die insgesamt betrachtet die Quintessenz der US-amerikanischen Gastronomie bilden: das Fastfood-Restaurant, der Western Saloon und die Billigkneipe (speakeasy). Hier wurden zwei ziemlich unterschiedliche Ambiente miteinander verbunden: der Heimservice- und Fastfood-Bereich – dort befindet sich ein Aluminium-Wandbild von Ronnie Cutrone, einem Mitarbeiter von Andy Warhol aus alten Zeiten – und die Bar im hinteren Bereich mit einer gänzlich anderen Atmosphäre. Dort herrschen Platten aus Stahl, Eiche und in Blautönen gefärbtes Glas vor.

Het ontwerp van dit hamburgerrestaurant verenigt drie aspecten die de essentie van de Amerikaanse gastronomie uitmaken: het fastfoodrestaurant, de westernsaloon en de speakeasy. Het etablissement combineert twee duidelijk gescheiden ruimten. Enerzijds, de thuisbezorging- en fastfoodzone, waar een aluminium muurdecoratie prijkt van Ronnie Cutrone, voormalig medewerker van Andy Warhol. In een heel andere sfeer, in de bar achteraan, overheersen de stalen platen, het eikenhout en het getint glas in blauwe kleurschakeringen.

El diseño de esta hamburguesería conjuga tres aspectos que representan la quintaesencia gastronómica norteamericana: el restaurante de comida rápida, el salón del oeste y el *speakeasy*. El establecimiento combina dos ambientes bien diferenciados. Por un lado, el servicio a domicilio y de comida rápida, que cuenta con un mural de aluminio de Ronnie Cutrone, antiguo colaborador de Andy Warhol, y, por el otro, el bar, situado al fondo de la planta, caracterizado por planchas de acero, roble y cristal tintado en tonos azules.

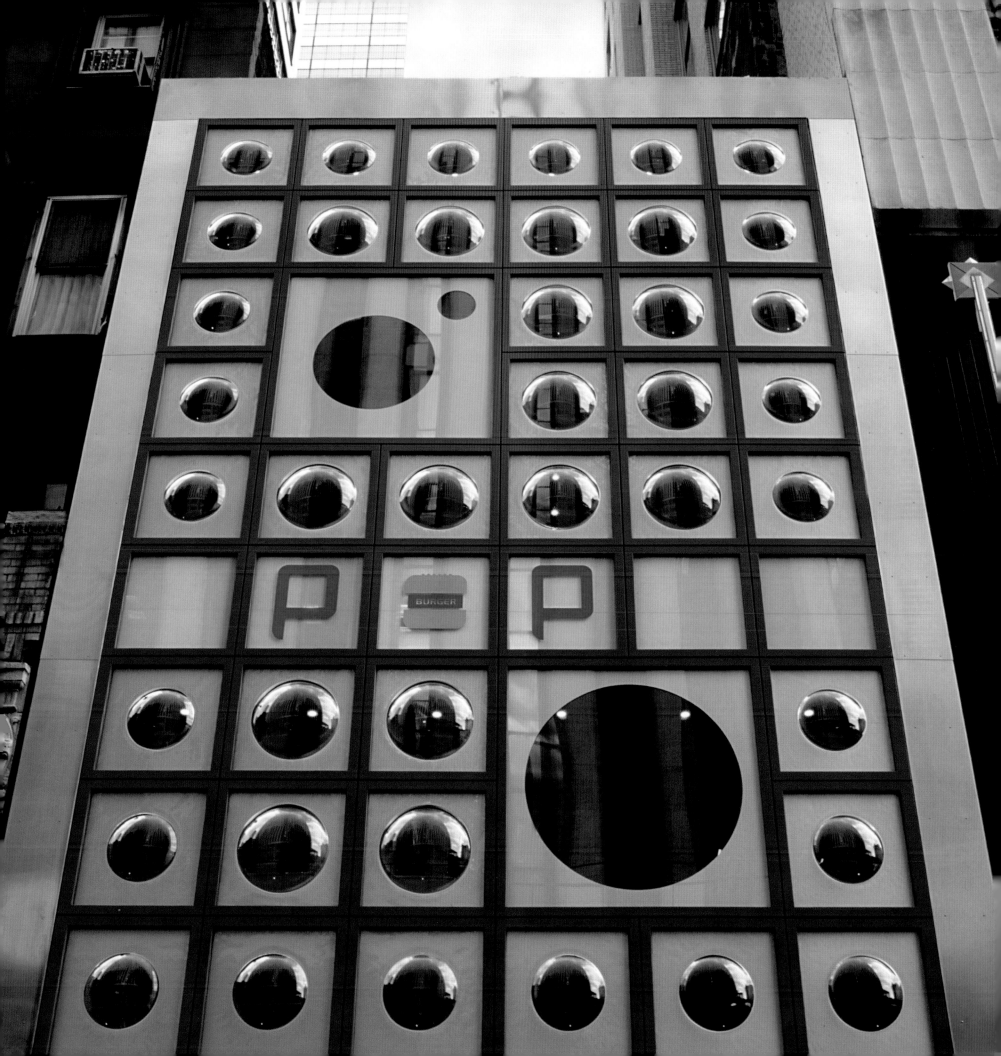

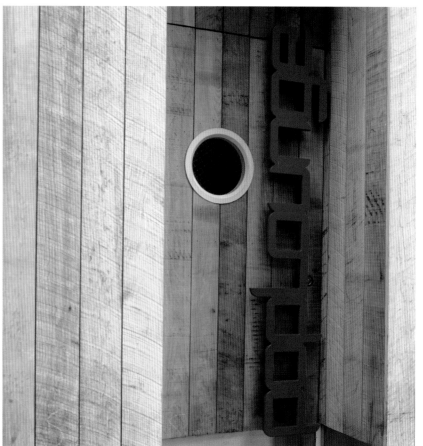

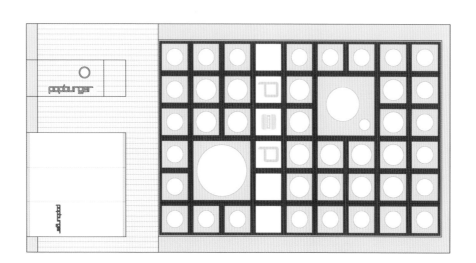

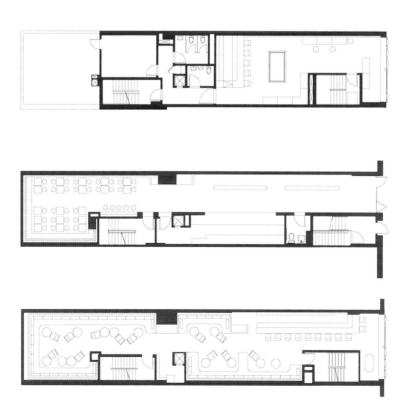

ALLEN + KILLCOYNE ARCHITECTS

Redken 3

The aim of this work was to stamp the Redken corporate image and character on its sales and marketing division. The shiny black receptionist's desk evokes the brand's product samples which are displayed on it for publicity purposes. A mural of the company's current ad campaign decorates the wall behind. The tinted glass coatings have the shiny look of a fashion magazine, while the floor is divided into small interconnected work areas that promote staff interaction.

L'objectif était ici de doter le service marketing et ventes de la marque Redken de caractère et d'une image cohérente avec l'entreprise. Le comptoir de la réception, avec sa surface noire et brillante, évoque les présentoirs de produits de la marque. Ces mêmes produits y sont d'ailleurs exposés à des fins publicitaires. Une reproduction de la campagne de publicité actuelle décore le mur qui se trouve derrière. Les revêtements de verre teinté rappellent l'aspect glacé des pages des magazines de mode. Les locaux se divisent en de nombreux petits espaces de travail, reliés entre eux afin de favoriser les interactions entre les employés.

Con quest'opera, l'obiettivo era quello di dare più carattere e una nuova immagine corporativa alla divisione di marketing e vendite della marca Redken. Il banco della reception, con la sua superficie nera lucida, evoca un campionario di prodotti della marca stessa, che vi sono esposti a fini pubblicitari. Un murale dell'attuale campagna di annunci della marca decora la parete che sorge proprio dietro. I rivestimenti di vetro colorato ricordano l'aspetto brillante delle pagine delle riviste di moda. Lo spazio è diviso in molte aree di lavoro di dimensioni ridotte, a loro volta intercomunicate per favorire l'interazione tra i lavoratori.

Das Ziel dieses Projektes war es, der Marketing- und Vertriebszweigstelle der Marke Redken Charakter und eine Corporate Identity zu verleihen. Die Rezeptionstheke mit ihrer schwarz glänzenden Oberfläche lässt an eine Musterkollektion von Produkten der Hausmarke denken, die dort zu Werbezwecken ausgestellt sind. Ein Bild der aktuellen Werbekampagne schmückt die hintere Wand, während die getönten Glasverkleidungen an die Seiten eines Hochglanz-Modemagazins erinnern lassen. Die Etage ist in viele kleinteilige Arbeitsbereiche unterteilt, die miteinander in Verbindung stehen, um die Zusammenarbeit und den Austausch unter den Beschäftigten zu begünstigen.

Het doel van dit werk was de marketing- en verkoopafdeling van het merk Redken karakter en bedrijfsimago te verschaffen. De receptiebalie, met een blinkend zwart oppervlak, evoqueert een productdisplay van het merk zelf waar bij wijze van reclame eigen producten uitgestald worden. Een muurdecoratie met foto's van de huidige reclamecampagne siert de achterliggende wand. De getinte glazen wanden doen denken aan het glanzende uitzicht van modetijdschriften. De etage wordt ingedeeld in kleine onderling verbonden werkruimten die interactie tussen de werknemers bevordert.

El objetivo de este proyecto era dotar de carácter y de una imagen coherente a la división de marketing y ventas de la marca Redken. El mostrador de recepción, con su superficie negra brillante, evoca un muestrario de productos de la propia marca, los cuales se exhiben en él con fines publicitarios. Un mural de la actual campaña de anuncios de la marca decora la pared que tiene justo detrás. Los revestimientos de cristal tintado recuerdan al aspecto brillante de las páginas de las revistas de moda. La planta se divide en muchas áreas de trabajo de tamaño reducido, a su vez interconectadas para propiciar la interacción de los trabajadores.

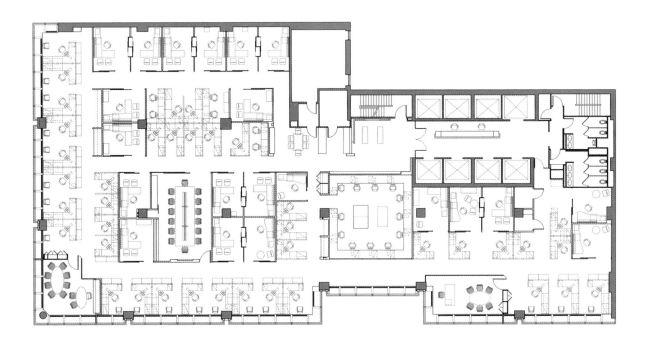

ALLEN + KILLCOYNE ARCHITECTS

Tenant Amenities

The project commissioned to the architects involved doing up the fourth floor of a residential property into a common area for use by all the owners and tenants: a spacious lounge room for watching television on a gigantic TV screen, a place to read by an impressive fireplace and an area to shoot some pool. The result is an interior space perfect for socializing which is both absolutely modern and at the same time a little retro and where one of the highlights is the stairwell, formed of a glass and stone box that distributes natural lighting to the different areas.

Le projet commandé aux architectes consistait à habiliter, au quatrième étage d'un immeuble résidentiel, un espace de zones communes pour tous les propriétaires et locataires : un grand lounge qui leur permettrait de regarder la télévision sur un écran géant, de lire près d'une imposante cheminée ou de jouer au billard. Le résultat est un lieu propice à l'interaction sociale, d'aspect furieusement moderne (avec une touche de rétro), où l'on remarque la cage d'escalier en verre et en pierre qui distribue un éclairage naturel aux différentes pièces qui l'entourent.

Il progetto richiesto agli architetti consisteva nell'abilitare, al quarto piano di un edificio residenziale, uno spazio di zone comuni che potessero usare tutti i proprietari e gli inquilini: un ampio lounge che permettesse loro di vedere la televisione in uno schermo gigante, di leggere accanto a un impressionante camino o giocare al biliardo. Il risultato è costituito da alcuni interni molto adatti alla socializzazione, dall'aspetto decisamente moderno (e anche un po' retro), nei quali spicca la tromba delle scale, formata da una scatola di vetro e pietra che distribuisce la luce naturale nelle varie stanze.

Das Projekt, das bei den Architekten in Auftrag gegeben wurde, bestand darin, im vierten Stock eines Wohnhauses einen Lebensraum zur gemeinsamen Nutzung zu schaffen. Alle Eigentümer und Mieter sollten die weiträumige Lounge nutzen können, in der man auf einem riesigen Bildschirm fernsehen, am Kamin lesen oder Billard spielen kann. Das Ergebnis sind Innenräume, die für das Gemeinschaftsleben prädestiniert sind, mit durch und durch moderner Ausstattung mit einem Touch zum Retro Style. Der Schacht für das Treppenhaus fällt auf: Er besteht aus einem Kasten aus Glas und Stein und sorgt für natürliche Belichtung in den verschiedenen Bereichen.

Het aan de architecten opgedragen project bestond erin op de vierde verdieping van een residentieel gebouw een gemeenschappelijke ruimte in te richten voor alle eigenaars en huurders: Een ruime lounge om op een reuzenscherm televisie te kijken, om te lezen bij een indrukwekkende open haard of om biljart te spelen. Het resultaat is een interieur dat perfect geschikt is voor socialisering, hypermodern met een retro-toets en als absolute blikvanger de traphal, een uit glas en steen gevormde box die het natuurlijk licht over de diverse vertrekken verdeelt.

El proyecto encargado a los arquitectos consistía en habilitar, en la cuarta planta de un edificio residencial, un espacio de zonas comunes que pudieran usar todos los propietarios e inquilinos: un amplio *lounge* que les permitiera ver la televisión en una pantalla gigante, leer junto a una impresionante chimenea o jugar al billar. El resultado son unos interiores muy propicios para la socialización, de aspecto rabiosamente moderno –a la vez que algo *retro*–, en los que destaca el hueco de las escaleras, formado por una caja de vidrio y piedra que distribuye la luz natural por las distintas estancias.

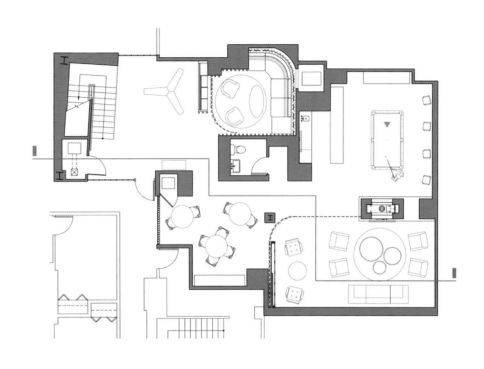

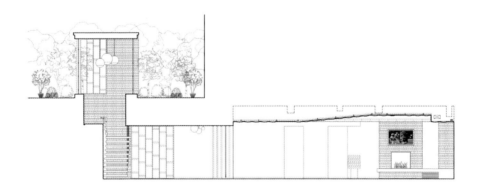

ALLIED WORKS ARCHITECTURE

Museum of Arts and Design

This project was denoted by the initial enthusiasm of the architects, who saw it as a chance to turn it into the city's architectural milestone in town. The aim behind the design was to underline the iconic presence of this 10-storey building and respond to the needs of the institution that will occupy it. The most noteworthy feature of the project is the terracotta and glass covering which evokes the principal theme of the collection, a look at different traditions in pottery art.

Ce projet a été marqué par l'enthousiasme des architectes, qui y ont tout de suite décelé un grand potentiel pour faire de ce bâtiment un monument architectural. L'intention était de renforcer la présence emblématique de ce volume de 10 étages et de répondre aux besoins de l'institution qui l'occupe. La caractéristique principale du projet est l'enveloppe de terre cuite et de verre qui recouvre le bâtiment et évoque le thème principal de la collection, un parcours à travers différentes traditions de l'art de la céramique.

Questo progetto è stato caratterizzato dall'iniziale entusiasmo degli architetti, che vi hanno visto delle magnifiche possibilità di trasformarlo in un vero e proprio simbolo architettonico della città. L'intenzione della proposta era quella di sottolineare la presenza iconica di questo volume di 10 piani, e rispondere alle necessità che l'istituzione ha di occuparlo. L'aspetto più notevole del progetto è la copertura di terracotta e cristallo, con la quale si evoca il tema principale della collezione, un percorso tra le varie tradizioni dell'arte della ceramica.

Der noch nicht fertiggestellte Entwurf wurde durch die Anfangsbegeisterung der Architekten geprägt, die darin ungeheure Möglichkeiten sahen, ihn zu einem architektonischen Meilenstein in der Stadt zu machen. Die Absicht bestand bei ihrem Vorschlag darin, die bildhafte Präsenz dieses Baukörpers mit seinen zehn Stockwerken zu unterstreichen und auf die Bedürfnisse der Institution, die es beherbergen soll, zu reagieren. Herausstechendes Merkmal des Entwurfs ist die Umhüllung mit Terrakotta und Glas, was an das Hauptthema der Sammlung erinnert, die einen Gang durch die verschiedenen Traditionen der keramischen Kunst umfasst.

Dit project werd gekenmerkt door het aanvankelijke enthousiasme van de architecten die er een ideale buitenkans in zagen om van het gebouw een architectonische mijlpaal te maken. De bedoeling van het ontwerp was de iconische waarde van dit uit 10 verdiepingen bestaande volume te benadrukken en aan de behoeften te voldoen van de institutie die het zou gaan bezetten. Het opvallendste aspect van het project is het uit terracotta en glas samengestelde omhulsel waarmee het hoofdthema van de collectie geëvoqueerd wordt, een route langsheen de keramiekkunst.

Este proyecto vino marcado por el entusiasmo de los arquitectos, que vieron en él unas tremendas posibilidades de convertirlo en un hito arquitectónico de la ciudad. La intención de la propuesta era la de resaltar la presencia icónica de este volumen de 10 plantas, y responder a las necesidades de la institución que había de ocuparlo. Lo más destacable del proyecto es la envoltura de terracota y cristal, que hace referencia al tema central de la colección, un recorrido por distintas tradiciones del arte de la cerámica.

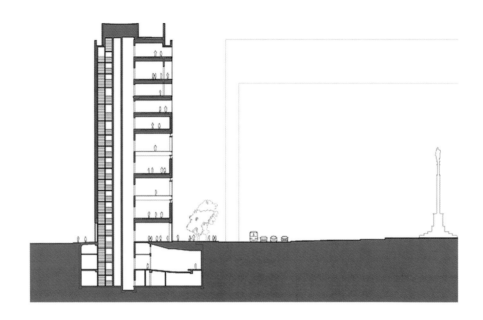

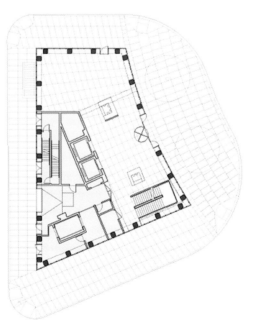

ARCHI-TECTONICS

V33 Residential Building

This indisputably original project involving a traditional building in the Tribeca neighborhood will have its sheets removed and replaced by a translucent stone and glass surface to give it a different look depending on the time of day. The joints and assembly work will barely be perceptible and the building will house spacious lofts with a great many terraces and outdoor areas that will merge organically with the interiors thanks to the new continuous rocky surface.

Pour ce projet à l'originalité indiscutable, un bâtiment traditionnel du quartier de Tribeca sera « délaminé ». Sa façade sera doublée d'une surface translucide en pierre et en verre dont l'aspect changera au cours de la journée. Les joints et le montage seront à peine perceptibles. L'immeuble abritera de vastes lofts dotés de nombreuses terrasses et d'espaces extérieurs qui fusionneront avec l'intérieur de façon organique grâce à la nouvelle surface continue en pierre.

In questo progetto, d'indiscutibile originalità, un edificio tradizionale del quartiere di Tribeca sarà «sfogliato». La sua facciata verrà ricoperta da una superficie semitrasparente di pietra e cristallo, diventando una superficie dall'aspetto cambiante secondo il momento della giornata, sulla quale saranno quasi impercettibili le giunture e gli assemblaggi. L'immobile ospiterà alcuni loft molto ampi, con diverse terrazze e spazi esterni che si fonderanno organicamente con gli interni grazie alla nuova superficie di pietra continua.

Dieser noch im Bau befindliche Entwurf von unbestreitbarer Originalität besteht darin, ein traditionelles Gebäude des Tribeca-Viertels zu „entblättern". Seine Fassade wird mit einer durchscheinenden Oberfläche aus Stein und Glas bedeckt. Sie wird je nach Tageszeit ihr Aussehen ändern, und ihre Verbindungsfugen und Montierungen werden kaum wahrnehmbar sein. In dem Bau werden großräumige Lofts untergebracht, mit etlichen Terrassen und Außenräumen, die dank der neuen durchgehenden Steinoberfläche organisch mit den Innenräumen verschmelzen.

In dit ontegensprekelijk origineel project, zal een traditioneel gebouw in de Tribeca-buurt van zijn laminaire structuur ontdaan worden. De gevel zal bekleed worden met een doorschijnend omhulsel, uit steen en glas, dat van uitzicht verandert naargelang het moment van de dag en een bijna voegloos oppervlak zonder assemblagesporen vertoont. Het gebouw zal zeer ruime lofts herbergen, met talrijke terrassen en buitenruimten die op organische wijze zullen fusioneren met de interieurs dankzij het nieuwe doorlopende, rotsachtige oppervlak.

Este original proyecto consiste en «deslaminar» un edificio tradicional del barrio de Tribeca y forrar la fachada con una superficie translúcida de piedra y cristal, para convertirla en una superficie de aspecto cambiante según la hora del día, en la que apenas serán perceptibles las juntas y ensamblajes. El inmueble acogerá *lofts* muy amplios, con muchas terrazas y espacios exteriores que se fusionarán orgánicamente con los interiores gracias a la nueva superficie pétrea ininterrumpida.

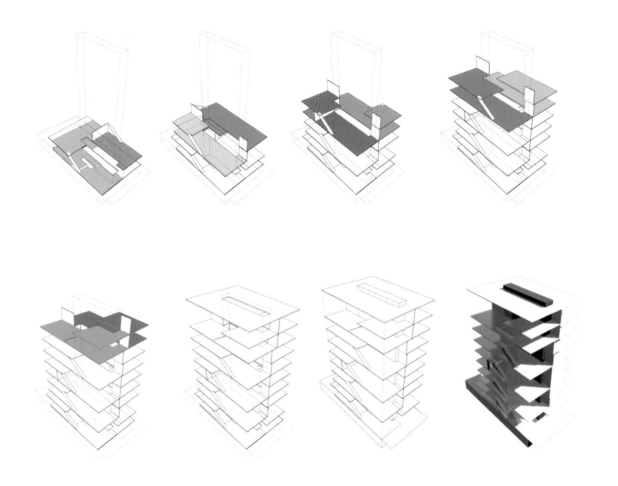

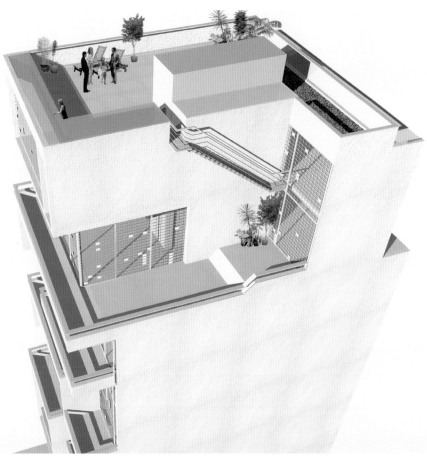

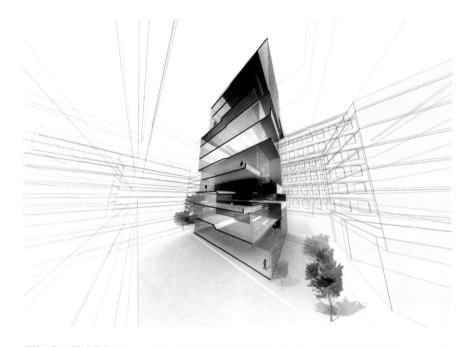

ARCHLAB

Tibi Boutique

This modern, casual boutique is located in the heart of Soho. Famous for its patterned garments with a '70s feel, the owners enlisted the architects to create a space that would help create a corporate image for the firm. Two structures with black and green canopies divide the store space and mark the route around it, while the space for the copper counters was also rehabilitated.

Cette boutique moderne et informelle se trouve au cœur de Soho. Elle est renommée pour ses vêtements imprimés inspirés des années 1970, et les propriétaires ont demandé aux architectes de créer un espace participant à la construction de leur image de marque. L'espace de la boutique est divisé par deux baldaquins verts et noirs. Ils définissent le parcours à suivre et mettent en valeur les comptoirs en cuivre.

Questa *boutique* moderna e disinvolta si trova nel pieno centro del quartiere di Soho. Famosa per i suoi capi fantasia con reminiscenze degli anni settanta, i suoi proprietari hanno chiesto agli architetti di progettare uno spazio che aiuti a creare un'immagine corporativa dell'azienda. A tale scopo, sono state concepite due strutture con baldacchino, in nero e verde, che separano lo spazio del negozio e fissano il percorso; nello stesso tempo, abilitano la zona destinata ai banconi con le casse.

Diese moderne Boutique liegt im Herzen von Soho. Berühmt für seine bedruckte Kleidung mit Reminiszenzen der 70er Jahre trugen die Eigentümer der Marke den Architekten die Aufgabe auf, einen Raum zu schaffen, der helfen sollte, ein Corporate Image für die Firma zu entwickeln. So wurden zwei abgehangene Decken in Schwarz- und Grüntönen konzipiert, die den Laden aufteilen und als Leitsystem fungieren; Gleichzeitig definieren sie den Kassenbereich.

Deze moderne en ongedwongen boetiek bevindt zich in het hart van Soho. De boetiek is beroemd om haar bedrukte jaren zeventig-kleding en de eigenaars wensten dat de architecten een ruimte zouden creëren die zou helpen vorm te geven aan het bedrijfsimago. Daarom werden twee structuren ontworpen met een overhuiving in zwart en groen die de winkelruimte verdeelt en als leidraad dient voor de bezoekers; terwijl tegelijkertijd ook de toonbankzone heringericht werd.

Esta moderna *boutique* de ropa casual se encuentra en el corazón del Soho. Famosa por sus prendas estampadas con reminiscencias de la década de 1970, los propietarios encomendaron a los arquitectos la tarea de crear un espacio que ayudara a reforzar la imagen corporativa de la firma. Dos estructuras con dosel, en tonos negro y verde, dividen la tienda y marcan el recorrido, al tiempo que configuran un el espacio para los mostradores de cobro.

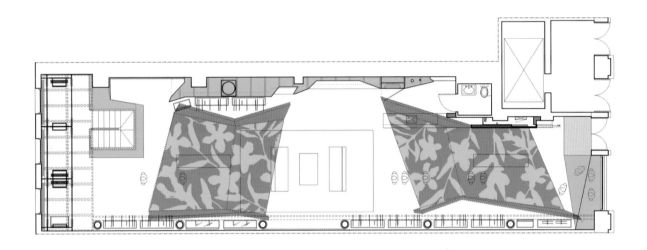

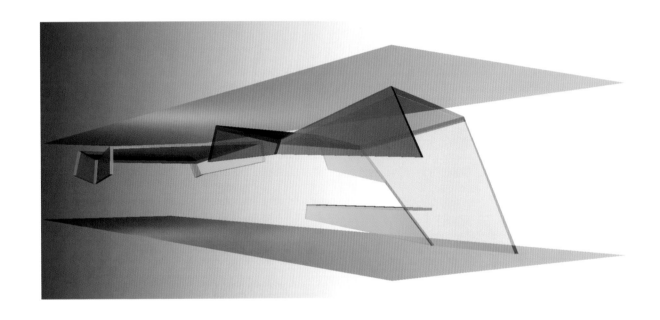

ARTHUR CASAS ARQUITETURA E DESIGN

Penthouse in Chelsea

The renovation of this apartment involved a very discrete combination of traditional materials like wicker and oak with a number of furniture design classics, such as the B&B chair, the Nakoshima armchair and the Vladimir Kogan coffee table, which spoke well of architect's meticulous selection process. He also personally took care of the design of the sofa. The lighting system is the work of the owner.

L'aménagement de cet appartement combine avec beaucoup de discrétion des matériaux traditionnels comme le rotin et le chêne et quelques pièces de mobilier très connues dans l'histoire du design, comme la chaise B&B, le fauteuil Nakoshima ou la table basse de Vladimir Kogan, ce qui prouve l'efficacité du méticuleux processus de sélection de l'architecte, qui s'est également chargé personnellement de la création du sofa. Le système d'éclairage est l'œuvre du propriétaire des lieux.

In questo appartamento si combinano in maniera molto discreta materiali tradizionali come il vimini e il legno di quercia nonché alcuni pezzi d'arredamento molto noti nella storia del design, come la sedia B & B, la poltrona Nakoshima o il tavolino da caffè di Vladimir Kogan, che costituiscono un'ottima testimonianza del meticoloso processo di selezione dell'architetto, il quale si è occupato personalmente anche del design del sofà. Il sistema d'illuminazione è invece opera del proprietario.

In diesem Apartment wurden auf ganz diskrete Weise traditionelle Materialien wie Korbgeflecht und Eichenholz mit einigen Möbelklassikern der Design-Geschichte kombiniert: Der B&B-Stuhl, der Nakoshima-Sessel und das Cafétischchen von Vladimir Kogan sprechen für die akribische Auswahl des Architekten, der persönlich das Design des Sofas übernahm. Die Verantwortung für das Beleuchtungssystem lag in den Händen des Eigentümers.

Voor de inrichting van dit appartement worden op discrete wijze traditionele materialen zoals rotan en eikenhout gecombineerd met enkele zeer bekende designstukken, zoals de stoel B & B, de zetel Nakoshima of de koffietafel van Vladimir Kogan, wat gunstig spreekt over het zorgvuldige selectieproces van de architect, die zich ook zelf inliet met het ontwerp van de sofa. Het verlichtingssysteem is het werk van de eigenaar zelf.

En el acondicionamiento de este apartamento se combinan de forma muy discreta materiales tradicionales como el mimbre y la madera de roble con algunas piezas clásicas del diseño, como la silla B & B, el sillón Nakoshima o la mesa de café de Vladimir Kogan, lo cual habla en favor del meticuloso proceso de selección del arquitecto, que también se encargó personalmente del diseño del sofá. El sistema de iluminación es obra del propietario.

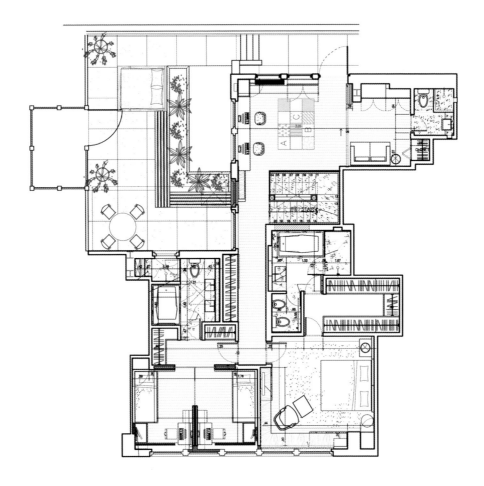

BONETTI/KOZERSKI STUDIO

Duplex Apartment

The renovation of the inside of this two-floor apartment close to Central Park has opened up space for the large living and dining rooms set around an impressive double-sided fireplace. Customized dark oak gives the floor a look of truly sober elegance, while a Cocobolo wood covering separates the stairwell from the living room. The combination of these tones with the travertine marble platform that surrounds the chimney is spectacular.

La rénovation intérieure de cet appartement de deux étages proche de Central Park a ouvert un vaste espace pour le salon et la salle à manger, qui s'articulent autour d'une impressionnante cheminée à deux faces. Un parquet artisanal en chêne foncé dote les sols d'une élégance très sobre, et un revêtement en bois de Cocobolo sépare la cage d'escalier du séjour. La combinaison de ces tons et de la plateforme en marbre travertin, qui entoure la cheminée, donne un résultat spectaculaire.

Il rinnovamento d'interni di questo appartamento a due piani vicino al Central Park ha creato lo spazio per un ampio soggiorno e una sala da pranzo che girano intorno a un incredibile camino a due lati. Un parquet artigianale di quercia scura dà al pavimento un'eleganza veramente sobria, mentre un rivestimento di legno di Cocobolo separa il vuoto delle scale del soggiorno. La combinazione di queste tonalità con la piattaforma di marmo travertino, che circonda il camino, risulta spettacolare.

Die Renovierung der Innenräume dieses zweistöckigen Apartments in der Nähe des Central Parks hat den Raum für einen weitläufigen Salon und ein Esszimmer geöffnet, die um einen beeindruckenden, nach zwei Seiten hin offenen Kamin angelegt sind. Ein dunkles Eichenparkett von kunsthandwerklicher Qualität verleiht den Böden eine geradezu nüchterne Eleganz, während eine Holzverkleidung aus Cocobolo den Treppenhausschacht vom Wohnraum trennt. Die Kombination dieser Farbtöne mit der Plattform aus Travertin, die den offenen Kamin umgibt, ist spektakulär.

De interieurrenovatie van dit appartement van twee verdiepingen dichtbij Central Park heeft ruimte vrij gemaakt voor een ruime zit- en eetkamer die werd ingericht rondom een indrukwekkende dubbelzijdige open haard. Het ambachtelijke donkere eikenhouten plankier verleent aan de vloer een zeer sobere elegantie, terwijl een houten Cocobolo bekleding het trapgat van de zitkamer scheidt. De combinatie van deze kleurschakeringen met het platform in travertijnmarmer die de open haard omgeeft is spectaculair.

La renovación de este apartamento de dos plantas cercano a Central Park ha abierto el espacio para un amplio salón y un comedor que figuran en torno a una impresionante chimenea de dos caras. Un entarimado artesanal de roble oscuro dota a los suelos de una elegancia realmente sobria, mientras que un revestimiento de madera de Cocobolo separa el hueco de las escaleras del cuarto de estar. La combinación de estos tonos con la plataforma de mármol travertino, que rodea la chimenea, resulta espectacular.

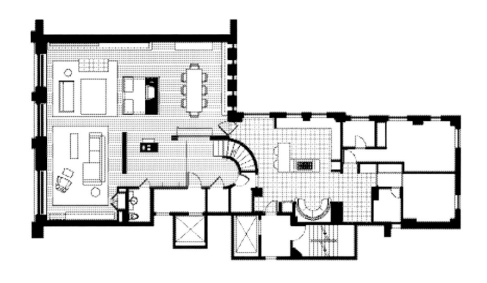

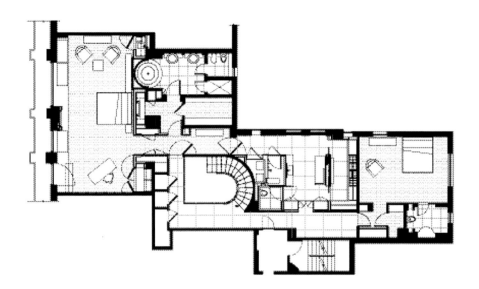

BONETTI/KOZERSKI STUDIO

Park West Apartment

Imposing spaces are the overriding feature of this home and accentuate the horizontal over vertical lines. The furniture and the few decorative, Asian-inspired elements provide a feeling of freedom and relaxation. This feeling is also embodied in the entire interior structure through the use of light colors. The variety of chosen materials highlights the simplicity of the design and contrasts with the furnishings.

Les espaces imposants prédominent dans cette habitation et accentuent davantage l'horizontalité plutôt que les lignes verticales. D'inspiration asiatique, le mobilier ainsi que le peu d'éléments décoratifs apportent une sensation de liberté et de relaxation. Cette sensation s'exprime également dans toute la structure intérieure, au travers des couleurs claires. La variété des matériaux sélectionnée se marie à la simplicité et contraste avec le mobilier.

In questa abitazione predominano spazi imponenti e orizzontalità rispetto alla verticalità. I mobili e i pochi arredi, di ispirazione orientale, trasmettono una sensazione di libertà e relax. Questa sensazione permane anche in tutta la struttura interna, grazie all'uso di colori chiari. La varietà di materiali selezionata si combina alla semplicità e crea un gioco di contrasti con i mobili.

In dieser Wohnung herrschen beeindruckende Platzverhältnisse, während das Waagerechte gegenüber den senkrechten Linien betont wurde. Die Möbel und die wenigen, asiatisch inspirierten Dekorationselemente bieten den Eindruck von Freiheit und Entspannung. Dieser Eindruck wird auch in der gesamten Innenstruktur anhand heller Farben wieder gegeben. Die Vielfalt der gewählten Materialien vereinigt sich mit der Schlichtheit und steht im Kontrast zum Mobiliar.

In deze woning overheersen imposante ruimten die veeleer de horizontaliteit dan de verticale lijnen benadrukken. Het meubilair en de luttele decoratieve elementen, met Aziatische inspiratie, zorgen voor een gevoel van vrijheid en ontspanning. Dit gevoel komt dankzij lichte kleuren tot uiting in de hele binnenstructuur. De verscheidenheid van de geselecteerde materialen wordt gecombineerd met eenvoud en contrasteert met het meubilair.

Imponentes espacios predominan en esta vivienda y ponen más énfasis en la horizontalidad que en las líneas verticales. El mobiliario y los pocos elementos decorativos, de inspiración asiática, brindan sensación de libertad y relajación. Esta sensación también se plasma en toda la estructura interior a través de los colores claros. La variedad de materiales seleccionada se une a la simplicidad y contrasta con el mobiliario.

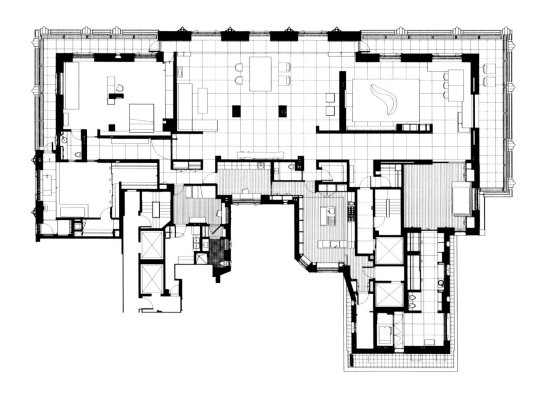

CCS ARCHITECTURE

Greenwich Village Condomine

The remodeling project for a Greenwich Village apartment is a good example of how to make the best use of limited space without having to extend. CCS Architecture transformed this old apartment by creating a micro-bedroom, carved from the main space by a wall. The home was designed to provide a single space that could be used for both eating and relaxing.

Cette rénovation d'un appartement de Greenwich Village illustre la manière d'exploiter au maximum l'espace restreint, sans besoin de mètres carré supplémentaires. CCS Architecture a transformé cet ancien appartement en créant une mini-chambre, isolée de l'espace principal par une cloison. Le logement a été aménagé de manière à créer un espace unique dans lequel il est possible de manger, se relaxer et travailler.

Questa ristrutturazione di un appartamento di Greenwich Village mostra come sfruttare al massimo uno spazio ridotto senza che sia necessario aggiungere metri quadrati. CCS Architecture ha trasformato questo vecchio appartamento creando una micro-camera da letto divisa dallo spazio principale da una parete. L'ambiente è stato organizzato in modo da creare uno spazio unico utilizzabile sia per mangiare e rilassarsi che per lavorare.

Diese Restaurierung eines Appartements in Greenwich Village ist ein Beispiel dafür, wie man einen kleinen Raum maximal nutzen kann, ohne Quadratmeter hinzuzufügen. CCS Architecture wandelte dieses alte Appartement um, indem ein Mikro-Schlafzimmer geschaffen wurde, das vom Hauptbereich durch eine Mauer getrennt ist. Die Wohnung wurde derart angepasst, dass ein einziger Raum zum Essen, Entspannen, wie auch zum Arbeiten geschaffen wurde.

Deze renovatie van een appartement in Greenwich Village is het voorbeeld van hoe een beperkte ruimte maximaal benut kan worden, zonder dat er vierkante meters aan toegevoegd hoeven te worden. CCS Architecture transformeerde dit oude appartement door een microslaapkamer te creëren, die van de hoofdruimte gescheiden werd door een muur. De woning werd zodanig ingericht dat een unieke ruimte ontstond die zowel kan dienen om er te eten, zich er te ontspannen en er te werken.

Esta renovación de un apartamento de Greenwich Village es el ejemplo de cómo aprovechar al máximo un espacio reducido, sin necesidad de añadir metros cuadrados. CCS Architecture transformó este apartamento antiguo creando un micro-dormitorio, dividido del espacio principal por una muralla. La vivienda se acondicionó para generar un espacio único aprovechable tanto para comer y relajarse como para trabajar.

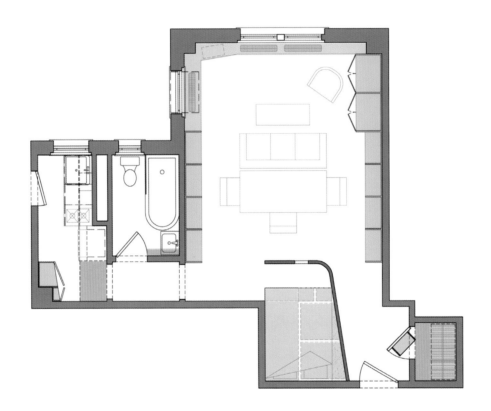

Loft in Cooper Square

This loft, originally a commercial premises, was turned into a home for a family of three. Priority was given to keeping the open-plan feel of the L-shaped space while creating private areas. As a result, the bedrooms were placed in the center and lined with wood to filter the sunlight. The anodized aluminum used in the kitchen acts as a light reflector.

Ce loft, originairement destiné à des fins commerciales, s'est transformé en un foyer pour une famille de trois personnes. La priorité consistait à maintenir le caractère ouvert de l'espace en forme de L, tout en créant des zones privées. Par conséquent, les chambres ont été installées au centre et recouvertes de bois permettant de filtrer la lumière du soleil. L'aluminium anodisé utilisé dans la cuisine agit comme réflecteur de la lumière.

Questo loft, originariamente utilizzato per scopi commerciali, si è trasformato nella casa di una famiglia composta da tre persone. La priorità era mantenere il carattere aperto dello spazio a forma di L e, nel contempo, creare delle zone private. Quindi al centro sono state sistemate le camere rivestite in legno che filtrano la luce del sole. L'alluminio anodizzato impiegato in cucina riflette la luce.

Dieses Loft, das ursprünglich zu geschäftlichen Zwecken genutzt wurde, wurde in ein Heim für eine dreiköpfige Familie verwandelt. Die Priorität lautete, den offenen Raumstil in L-Form beizubehalten und gleichzeitig Privatbereiche zu schaffen. Somit wurden die holzverkleideten Schlafzimmer, die das Sonnenlicht filtern, in die Mitte gelegt. Das in der Küche eingesetzte eloxierte Aluminium reflektiert das Licht.

Deze loft -oorspronkelijk gebruikt voor commerciële doeleinden- werd omgevormd tot een thuis voor een gezin met drie leden. De prioriteit bestond erin het open karakter van de ruimte in L-vorm te behouden en tegelijkertijd privézones te creëren. Daarom werden in het midden de slaapkamers geïnstalleerd, bekleed met houten panelen die het zonlicht filteren. Het geanodiseerd aluminium dat in de keuken gebruikt werd, werkt als lichtreflector.

Este loft -originariamente usado con fines comerciales- se transformó en el hogar de una familia de tres miembros. La prioridad era mantener el carácter abierto del espacio en forma de L y, a la vez, crear zonas privadas. Por tanto, se instalaron en el centro los dormitorios revestidos de madera que filtran la luz del sol. El aluminio anodizado que se empleó en la cocina actúa como reflector de la luz.

DESAI/CHIA ARCHITECTURE

Renovated Loft

Previously dark and cavernous interior spaces were painstakingly reformed with spectacular results: the new areas in this apartment are very open and well lit. Two clearly differentiated sections running perpendicularly to each other permit the separation of public and private areas. The kitchen has an elongated bench that groups together the cooking and washing activities and provides a space which can be used to eat at.

Avant sa rénovation, la principale caractéristique de ce loft était qu'il ressemblait à une caverne obscure. Le résultat des travaux est spectaculaire, et les nouveaux espaces sont dégagés et bien éclairés. Deux parties bien différenciées orientées perpendiculairement l'une par rapport à l'autre permettent de séparer les zones publiques des zones privées. La cuisine est dotée d'une console allongée qui centralise les activités de cuisine et de lavage, et offre un espace qui fait office de coin-repas.

Gli interni che prima richiamavano l'attenzione per essere oscuri e cavernosi sono stati coscientemente restaurati con risultati spettacolari (nuovi spazi molto diafani e bene illuminati) in questo appartamento. Due sezioni ben differenziate, orientate perpendicolarmente una rispetto all'altra, permettono la separazione degli ambiti pubblici da quelli privati. La cucina ha una console allungata in cui si svolgono le attività di preparazione dei cibi e di lavaggio, e offre a sua volta uno spazio che fa le veci di una sala da pranzo.

Die dunklen, fast höhlenartigen Innenräume dieses Apartments wurden gewissenhaft umgebaut. Das Ergebnis ist spektakulär: neue lichtdurchflutete und gut beleuchtete Räume. Zwei grundverschiedene Bereiche, die im rechten Winkel zueinander stehen, erlauben es, die Gemeinschaftszone von den Privaträumen zu trennen. Die Küche besitzt einen lang gestreckten Küchenblock, der Herd und Spüle zusammenfasst und zugleich Raum bietet, der als Essbereich dient.

Interieurs die vroeger de aandacht trokken omdat ze donker en spelonkachtig waren, werden in dit appartement zorgvuldig verbouwd en wel met spectaculaire resultaten -nieuwe transparante en goed verlichte ruimten-. Twee duidelijk onderscheiden delen die loodrecht tegenover elkaar staan maken het mogelijke de openbare vertrekken van de privévertrekken te scheiden. De keuken beschikt over een lang aanrecht dat de kook- en afwasactiviteiten verenigt en tegelijkertijd een ruimte biedt die tevens dienst doen als eetkamer.

Los interiores de este apartamento que antes llamaban la atención por oscuros y cavernosos han sido reformados con espectaculares resultados: nuevos espacios muy diáfanos y bien iluminados. Dos secciones bien diferenciadas orientadas perpendicularmente una con respecto a la otra permiten separar los espacios públicos de los privados. La cocina cuenta con una consola alargada que agrupa las actividades de cocina y lavado, y ofrece a su vez un espacio que hace las veces de comedor.

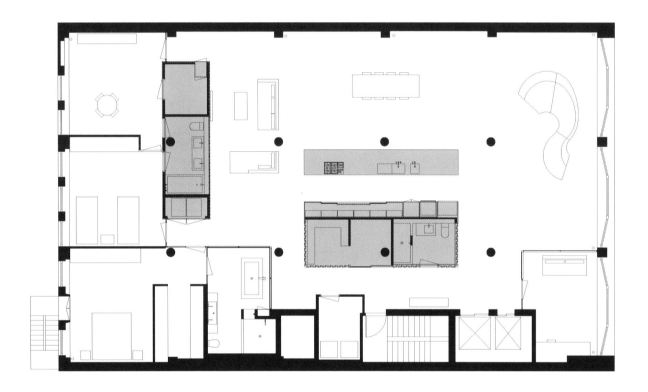

ELMSLIE OSLER

Amaridian

This space designed by Elmslie Osler acts as a store and, at the same time, an exhibition space for South African art. The design, in ocher tones and matt textures, evokes the features of the African landscape as well as its local crafts. A long wall of prefabricated paper compounds determines the configuration of the floor, with room for the large showcase that contains most of the works on display. Behind the wall, a darker corridor ushers the visitor into a space that displays the collection along a more rambling route.

Cet espace conçu par Elmslie Osler est en même temps un magasin et une salle d'exposition d'art sud-africain. La décoration en tons ocres avec des textures mates évoque les caractéristiques du paysage africain et de l'artisanat local. Un long mur de plaques de papier aggloméré préfabriquées donne la structure des locaux, et abrite une grande vitrine qui contient la plus grande partie des objets exposés. Derrière ce mur, un couloir plus obscur invite les visiteurs à explorer les objets dans un parcours plus labyrinthique.

Lo spazio concepito da Elmslie Osler funziona come negozio e, nello stesso tempo, come luogo d'esposizione dell'arte sudafricana. Il design, con tonalità ocra e texture opache, evoca le caratteristiche del paesaggio africano, così come quelle dell'artigianato della zona. Una parete allungata, fatta di composti prefabbricati di carta, fissa la distribuzione del piano, con uno spazio per la grande vetrina che contiene la maggior parte dei pezzi esposti. Dietro questo muro, un corridoio più scuro invita il visitante a circondarsi delle opere artigianali in un percorso più labirintico.

Der Raum, der von Elmslie Osler konzipiert wurde, hat die Funktion eines Ladens und zugleich eines Ausstellungsraums für südafrikanische Kunst. Das Design mit seinen dunklen Tönen und matten Texturen erinnert an die Charakteristika der afrikanischen Landschaft ebenso wie an das Kunsthandwerk aus diesen Breitengraden. Eine Wand aus vorgefertigten Papierelementen bestimmt die Gestaltung des Bodens. Vitrinen und Schaukästen wurden in dieser Wand eingelassen, um den Großteil der Exponate zu präsentieren. Dahinter befindet sich ein dunklerer Korridor, der den Besucher zu einem Rundgang durch die weitere Ausstellung einlädt.

De ruimte die door Elmslie Osler ontworpen werd, functioneert tegelijkertijd als winkel en tentoonstellingsruimte voor Zuid-Afrikaanse kunst. Het ontwerp, met okertinten en matte texturen, evoqueert de kenmerken van het Afrikaanse landschap en van het lokale ambachtswerk. Een lange wand uit geprefabriceerde papierplaten bepalen de configuratie van de etage, waarin een grote vitrine geplaatst werd met het grootste deel van de tentoongestelde stukken. Achter deze muur nodigt een donkerdere gang de bezoeker uit zich in een soort doolhof met ambachtswerk te omringen.

El espacio concebido por Elmslie Osler funciona como tienda y a la vez como lugar de exposición de arte sudafricano. El diseño, con tonos ocres y texturas mates, evoca el paisaje y la artesanía africanos. Una alargada pared de conglomerado de papel determina la configuración de la planta, con cabida para la gran vitrina que contiene la mayor parte de los objetos expuestos. Detrás de este muro, un pasillo más oscuro invita al visitante a conocer la colección de artesanía en un recorrido más laberíntico.

GHISLAINE VIÑAS INTERIOR DESIGN

Chelsea Gallery

Transforming this ruin into a modern art gallery posed two challenges for the interior designer and the architects: how to get a good space both for exhibiting artwork and for hosting openings and how to escape from the color white that usually predominates in galleries. They came up with the idea of different shades of green as a chromatic counterpoint in the bathroom, offices and warehouses. The rounded corners and aluminum sheets on the ceiling help delimit the routes for visitors.

La décoratrice d'intérieurs et les architectes devaient transformer un espace en ruines en une galerie d'art moderne. Ils ont été confrontés à un double défi : obtenir un espace tout aussi adapté à l'exposition d'œuvres d'art qu'à l'organisation de vernissages, et imaginer une décoration qui se distingue du blanc omniprésent habituel dans ce type d'établissement. C'est ainsi qu'apparut l'idée d'utiliser plusieurs tons de vert, comme contrepoint chromatique dans les toilettes, les bureaux et les pièces d'entreposage. Les coins arrondis et les bandes d'aluminium du plafond aident à indiquer le parcours aux visiteurs.

La trasformazione di uno spazio in rovina di una moderna galleria d'arte è stata intrapresa dalla designer d'interni e dagli architetti con una doppia sfida: quella di ottenere uno spazio adatto tanto alla mostra di opere d'arte quanto a fare da sfondo per le inaugurazioni, e apportare qualcosa di diverso dal normale uso del colore bianco che predomina in stabilimenti dello stesso tipo. In tal modo è nata l'idea del verde, in varie tonalità, come contrappunto cromatico nel bagno, negli uffici e nei luoghi di magazzino. Gli angoli arrotondati e le lamine d'alluminio del soffitto aiutano il visitatore a seguire i percorsi.

Die Umgestaltung eines verfallenen Gebäudes in eine moderne Kunstgalerie wurde von der Innenarchitektin und den Architekten als Antwort auf eine doppelte Herausforderung vorgenommen: Sie bestand darin, einen Raum zu schaffen, der für die Präsentation von Kunst ebenso geeignet sein sollte wie für die Vernissagen; auch sollte der Dominanz der Farbe Weiß in Galerien etwas entgegengesetzt werden. So entstand die Idee, unterschiedliche Grüntöne als farbliches Gegengewicht in Bad, Büroräumen und Lager unterzubringen. Die abgerundeten Ecken und die Alubleche an der Decke tragen dazu bei, den Rundweg für den Besucher zu markieren.

De transformatie van een vervallen ruimte in een moderne kunstgalerij vertegenwoordigde voor de binnenhuisarchitecte en de architecten een dubbele uitdaging: een ideale ruimte creëren om kunst tentoon te stellen dat tevens als kader kan dienen voor de inhuldigingen. Bovendien wilden ze ontsnappen aan de kleur wit dat gewoonlijk in dit soort lokalen overheerst. Zo ontstond het idee om als chromatisch contrast, verschillende groenschakeringen te gebruiken in de badkamer, de kantoren en de bergplaatsen. De afgeronde hoeken en aluminium platen helpen de bezoeker de te volgen weg te vinden.

La transformación de un espacio en ruinas en una moderna galería de arte fue acometida por la interiorista y los arquitectos con un reto doble: el de lograr un espacio idóneo para las exposiciones de arte y las inauguraciones, y a la vez aportar algo distinto al habitual predominio del blanco en este tipo de salas. Fue así como surgió la idea del verde, en distintas tonalidades, como contrapunto cromático en el baño, las oficinas y los lugares de almacenamiento. Las esquinas redondeadas y las láminas de aluminio del techo ayudan a marcar los recorridos al visitante.

PRINT PORTFOLIO 2005

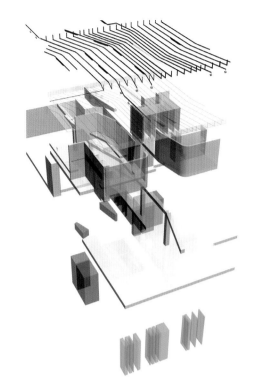

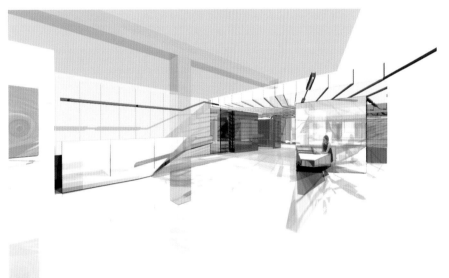

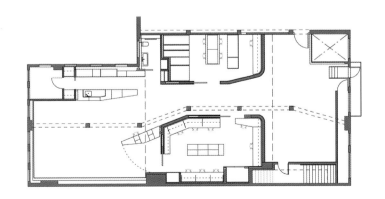

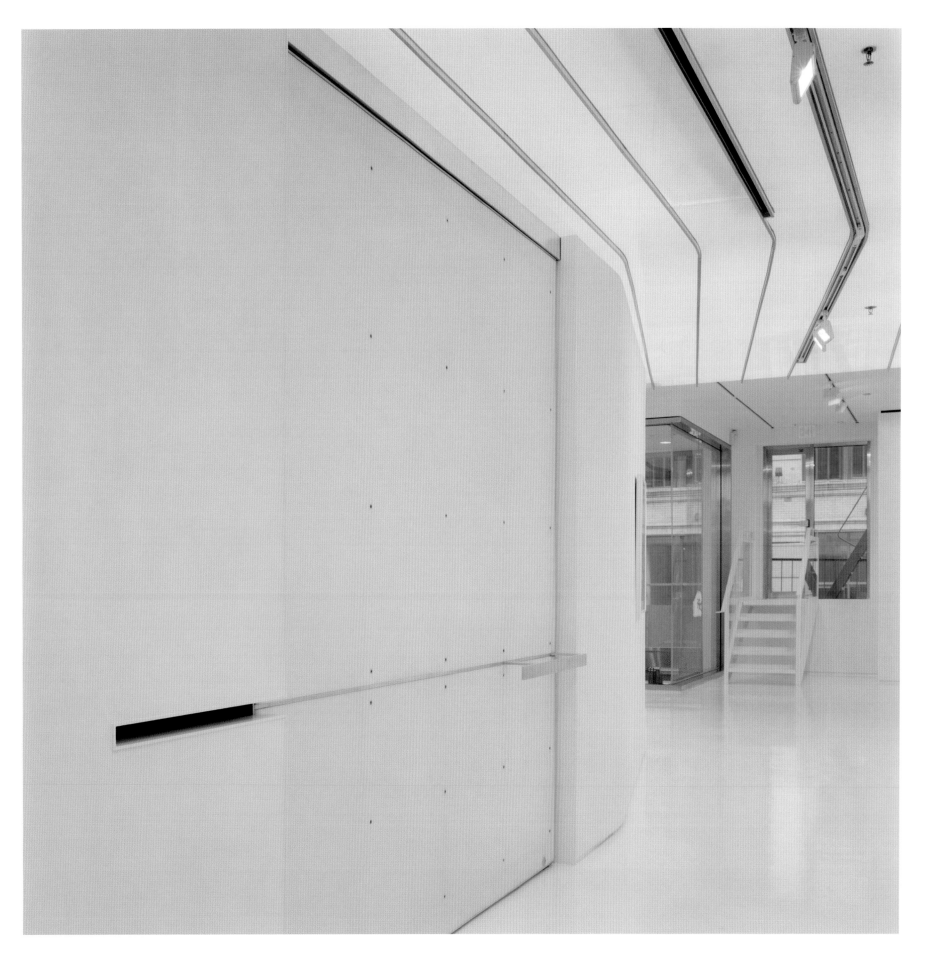

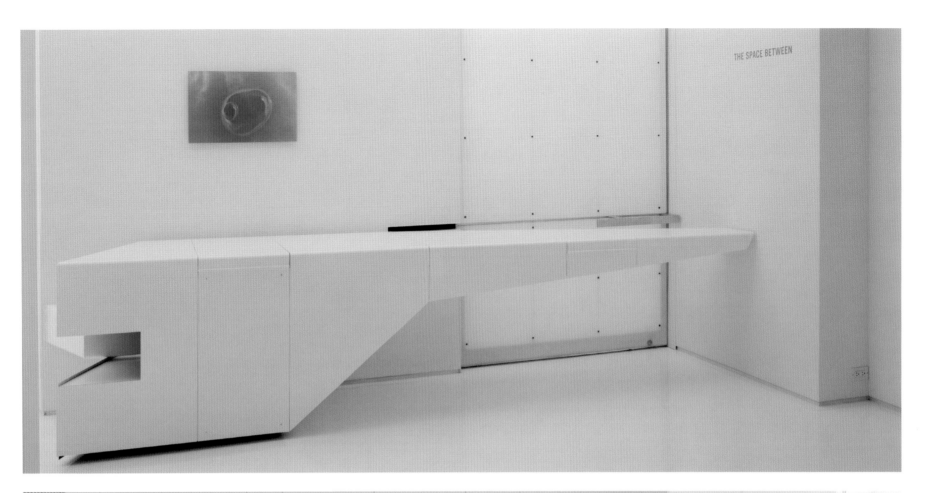

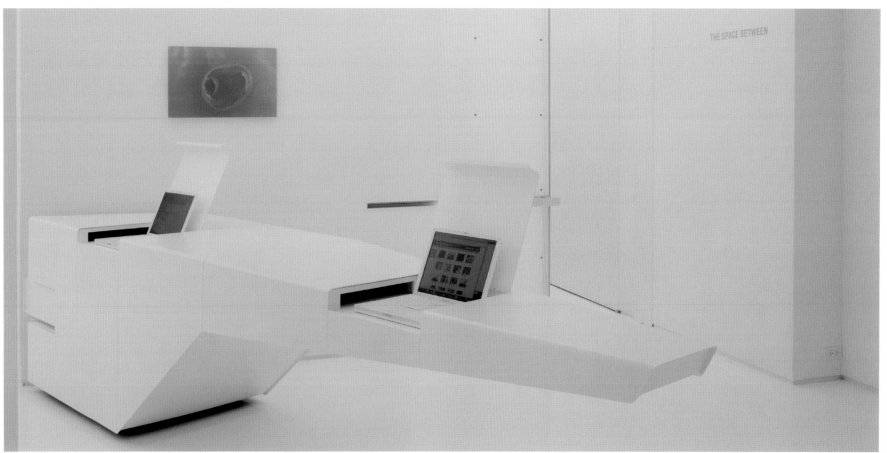

THE SPACE BETWEEN

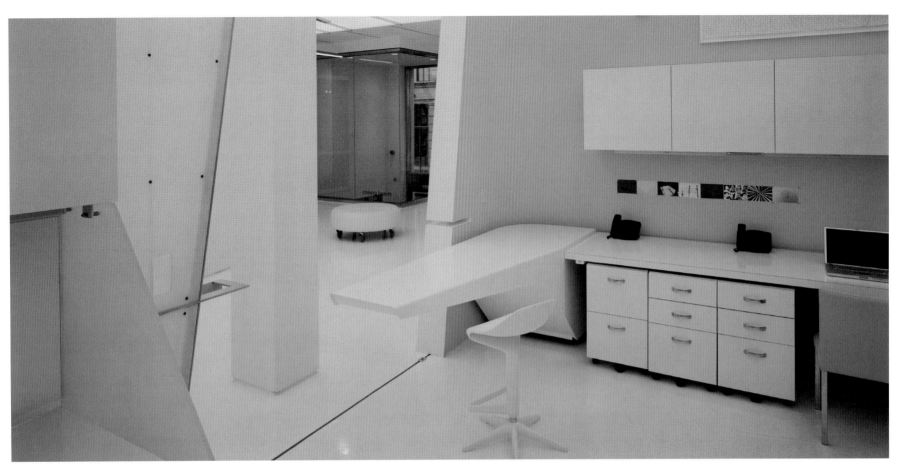

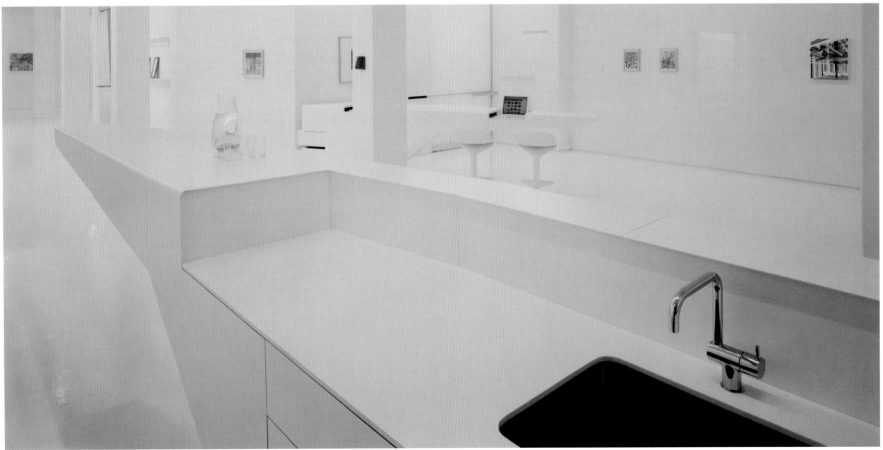

Juan Valdez Flagship Café

As this is the first store of a franchise that aims to expand across the US, the omnipresence of the coffee-shop's brand logo marked the project indisputably. The façade, the building's main attraction, aims to link the Colombian and American cultures, with an impressive wooden wall that presents the building and connects the coffee shop with the bean store. The undulating wall that runs the length of the establishment is evocative of coffee in its liquid state and illuminated by a light positioned in a hidden source.

Comme il s'agit de la première boutique d'une franchise qui souhaite se multiplier aux États-Unis, l'omniprésence du logo de cette marque de café est l'une des caractéristiques les plus frappantes du projet. La façade, principale réclame du bâtiment, est conçue pour établir un lien entre les cultures colombienne et nord-américaine, avec un imposant mur en bois qui présente l'immeuble et relie le bar et la boutique de café en grains. Le mur ondulant qui court le long de l'établissement évoque le café dans son état liquide, et est avantageusement éclairé par une source de lumière dissimulée.

Dal momento che si tratta della prima sede di un franchising che intende moltiplicarsi negli Stati Uniti, l'onnipresenza del logo di questa marca di caffè ha condizionato indiscutibilmente il progetto. La facciata, ossia il principale elemento promozionale dell'edificio, intende servire da legame tra la cultura colombiana e quella nordamericana, con un imponente muro di legno che presenta lo stabile e mette in comunicazione la caffetteria con il negozio. La parete ondulante, che percorre in senso longitudinale lo stabilimento, ricorda la l'aspetto del caffè allo stato liquido, ed è adeguatamente illuminata da una sorgente di luce nascosta.

Da es sich hierbei um den ersten Sitz des Franchise-Unternehmens Juan Valdez Café handelt, das sich in den USA ausdehnen möchte, ist das Projekt zweifellos durch die Allgegenwärtigkeit des Logos dieser Kaffeemarke bestimmt. Die Fassade mit einer beeindruckenden Holzwand ist die Hauptattraktion des Gebäudes; sie präsentiert es und verbindet das Café mit dem Kaffeegeschäft. Dabei versucht sie, als Verbindung zwischen kolumbianischer und nordamerikanischer Kultur zu dienen. Die entlang der Niederlassung verlaufende gewellte Wand soll die Eigenschaft des Kaffees in flüssigem Zustand darstellen und wird von hinten beleuchtet.

Aangezien dit het eerste filiaal betreft van een franchise die zich in heel de Verenigde Staten wenst te vestigen, werd het project onbetwistbaar gekenmerkt door de alomtegenwoordigheid van het merklogo. De gevel, de belangrijkste blikvanger van het gebouw, streeft ernaar met een imposante houten muur, die het gebouw voorstelt en de koffieshop met de bonenwinkel verbindt, als verbindingselement te dienen tussen de Colombiaanse en Noord-Amerikaanse cultuur. De golvende wand die in de lengte het etablissement doorloopt, evoqueert de vloeibare toestand van de koffie en wordt op passende wijze verlicht door een verscholen lichtbron.

Al tratarse de la primera sede de una franquicia que pretende multiplicarse por Estados Unidos, la omnipresencia del logotipo de esta marca cafetera marcó indiscutiblemente el proyecto. La fachada, principal reclamo del edificio, pretende servir de vínculo entre las culturas colombiana y norteamericana, con un imponente muro de madera que presenta el inmueble y conecta la cafetería con la tienda de grano. La pared ondulante que recorre longitudinalmente el establecimiento evoca la propiedad del café en su estado líquido, convenientemente iluminada por una luz de fuente oculta.

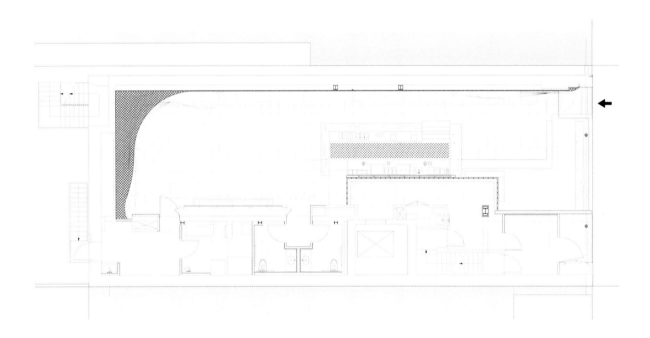

HARIRI & HARIRI ARCHITECTURE

Page Residence

Upon entering this Carnegie Hill apartment there is a hall running north to south that connects the different rooms. The bedrooms are found on the western side, with large wengue doors. The living room, dining room and library are interconnected by translucent sheets on the wall and sliding panels that encourage the feeling of space. The idea when choosing objects and materials was to generate an impression of elegance and refinement – a feat ably achieved.

Une galerie court du nord au sud depuis l'entrée de cet appartement de Carnegie Hill et relie les différentes pièces du logement. Les chambres se trouvent dans la partie occidentale, et sont dotées d'imposantes portes en bois de Wengué. Le séjour, la salle à manger et la bibliothèque sont reliés entre eux par des plaques murales translucides et des panneaux coulissants, qui renforcent la sensation d'espace. La sélection d'objets et de matériaux vise à générer une impression d'élégance et de raffinement, avec un succès indiscutable.

Quando si entra in questo appartamento di Carnegie Hill, una galleria va da nord a sud, collegando le varie stanze della casa. Le camere si trovano nella parte occidentale, con imponenti porte di legno di wengue. Il soggiorno, la sala da pranzo e la biblioteca sono collegati tra loro mediante lamine di parete semitrasparente e pannelli scorrevoli, rafforzando la sensazione d'ampiezza. Nella scelta di oggetti e materiali si è cercato di produrre un'impressione di eleganza e raffinatezza, con un successo indiscutibile.

Wenn man dieses Apartment in Carnegie Hill betritt, erstreckt sich in Nord-Süd-Richtung eine Galerie, die die verschiedenen Zimmer der Wohnung miteinander verbindet. Die Schlafzimmer mit imposanten Wengeholztüren befinden sich im Westteil. Das Wohnzimmer, das Esszimmer und die Bibliothek sind durch mobile Paneele und transluzente Wandpaneele und durchscheinende Wandpaneele verbunden, was ein Gefühl von Weitläufigkeit vermittelt. Bei der Auswahl der Einzelgegenstände und Materialien versuchte man, den Eindruck von Eleganz und Raffinesse zu erzeugen. Das ist unzweifelhaft gelungen.

Wanneer men dit appartement in Carnegie Hill binnenkomt, strekt zich van noord tot zuid een gang uit die de diverse vertrekken van het huis verbindt. De slaapkamers, met indrukwekkende deuren in wengéhout, liggen in het westelijke deel. De zitkamer, de eetkamer en de bibliotheek zijn onderling met elkaar verbonden door doorschijnende wand- en schuifpanelen waardoor het ruimtegevoel versterkt wordt. Bij de selectie van de voorwerpen en materialen werd ernaar gestreefd een elegante en verfijnde indruk te wekken, en daar werd absoluut in geslaagd.

Al entrar en este apartamento de Carnegie Hill, una galería se extiende de norte a sur, conectando las distintas estancias del hogar. Los dormitorios se encuentran en la parte occidental, con imponentes puertas de madera de wengué. El cuarto de estar, el comedor y la biblioteca están interconectados por láminas de pared translúcida y paneles correderos, reforzando la sensación de amplitud. En la selección de objetos y materiales se ha buscado generar una impresión de elegancia y refinamiento, con indiscutible éxito.

JAMES SLADE/SLADE ARCHITECTURE

Flatiron Apartment

This rectangular loft was divided into two areas – a private space at one end, and a public space at the other. The kitchen and bathroom were placed at the center. The clients' brief was that furnishings and objects were to be integrated in the décor scheme, and that the apartment should be functional for city living.

Ce loft rectangulaire a été divisé en deux zones, une partie privée d'un côté et une partie publique de l'autre, la cuisine et la salle de bain se situant au cœur de l'habitation. La consigne fixée par les occupants était que les objets et les meubles fassent partie intégrante de la décoration et que l'appartement soit fonctionnel et adapté au rythme de vie urbain.

Questo *loft* rettangolare è stato diviso in due aree, una privata su un'estremità e una pubblica sul lato opposto. Cucina e bagno sono stati ubicati al centro. La condizione posta dagli abitanti della casa era che gli oggetti e i mobili fossero integrati nell'arredamento e che l'appartamento fosse funzionale ai ritmi di vita urbani.

Dieses rechteckige *Loft* wurde in zwei Bereiche, d. h., in einen privaten Bereich an einem Ende und einen öffentlichen Bereich auf der gegenüberliegenden Seite, geteilt. Küche und Bad wurden in die Mitte gelegt. Die Vorgabe der Bewohner lautete, dass Gegenstände und Möbel in die Ausstattung integriert sein sollten und das Appartement im Rhythmus des Stadtlebens Lebens funktionell sein sollte.

Deze *rechthoekige loft* werd in twee zones opgedeeld, een privédeel aan één uiteinde en het openbare deel aan het tegenovergestelde uiteinde. De keuken en de badkamer werden in het midden geïnstalleerd. De opdracht van de bewoners bestond erin de voorwerpen en meubels in de decoratie te integreren om een functioneel appartement te creëren dat aangepast zou zijn aan het ritme van het stadsleven.

Este *loft* rectangular fue dividido en dos áreas, una privada en uno de los extremos y una zona pública en el lado opuesto. La cocina y el cuarto de baño se situaron en el medio. La consigna que establecieron los habitantes era que los objetos y los muebles estuvieran integrados a la decoración, y fuera un apartamento funcional al ritmo de vida urbano.

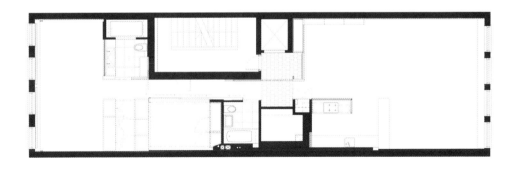

JAMES SLADE/SLADE ARCHITECTS

Hochhauser Residence

This central New York home is the result of an integral remodeling project involving two early 1960s apartments. The new project included a complete restructuring of the interior layout, maximizing storage space, and enhancing city views, especially over the south and west.

Situé au cœur de New York, ce logement est le fruit de la rénovation intégrale de deux appartements anciens, datant du début des années 60 du siècle dernier. Le nouveau projet prévoyait une réorganisation complète de l'espace intérieur, l'optimisation des espaces de rangement et l'exploitation des vues sur la ville, surtout celles donnant au sud et à l'ouest.

Questa casa, ubicata nel centro di New York, è il risultato della ristrutturazione completa di due vecchi appartamenti risalenti all'inizio degli anni '60. Il nuovo progetto prevedeva una riorganizzazione totale degli spazi interni, l'ottimizzazione delle zone di contenimento e la possibilità di godere del panorama sulla città, soprattutto verso sud e ovest.

Diese im Zentrum von New York gelegene Wohnung ist das Ergebnis einer kompletten Reform zwei alter Appartements vom Anfang der siebziger Jahre des vergangenen Jahrhunderts. Das neue Projekt sah die komplette Neugestaltung des Innenraums, die Optimierung der Aufbewahrungsbereiche und die Nutzung der Aussichten auf die Stadt - insbesondere Richtung Süden und Westen - vor.

Deze woning, gelegen in het centrum van New York, is het resultaat van de volledige verbouwing van twee oude appartementen die dateren uit het begin van de jaren zestig van de vorige eeuw. Het nieuwe project voorzag een volledige reorganisatie van de binnenruimte, de optimalisatie van de opslagruimten en de optimale benutting van het uitzicht op de stad, vooral naar het zuiden en het westen toe.

Esta vivienda, ubicada en el centro de Nueva York, es el resultado de la reforma integral de dos antiguos apartamentos que datan de principios de la década de 1970. El nuevo proyecto supuso una completa reorganización del espacio interior, la optimización de las zonas de almacenamiento y el aprovechamiento de las vistas a la ciudad, especialmente hacia el sur y el oeste.

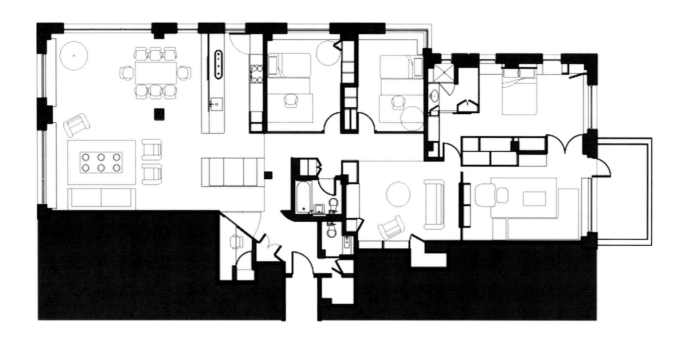

JAMES SLADE/SLADE ARCHITECTURE

Noho Loft

This apartment was designed for a photographer who needed space to organize and store part of his work. The high ceilings enabled good use to be made of the space. Windows were placed on one wall, and the apartment was laid out to create spaces that blocked light from reaching others.

Cet appartement a été conçu pour un photographe ayant besoin d'espace pour classer et conserver une partie de son travail. La hauteur des plafonds a permis de tirer profit au mieux de la pièce. Grâce à l'installation des fenêtres sur un seul mur, l'appartement a été organisé de manière à permettre la création d'espaces obstruant le passage de la lumière vers d'autres secteurs de l'habitation.

Questo appartamento è stato progettato per un fotografo che aveva bisogno di spazio per achiviare e conservare parte del suo lavoro. I soffitti alti hanno consentito di sfruttare al massimo l'ambiente. Con le finestre sistemate lungo un'unica parete, l'appartamento è stato organizzato in modo tale da generare spazi che non ostruissero il passaggio della luce verso gli altri settori.

Dieses Appartement wurde für einen Fotografen mit Platzbedarf zur Ablage und Aufbewahrung eines Teils seiner Arbeit entworfen. Die hohen Decken ermöglichten eine gute Raumnutzung. Anhand der Anordnung der Fenster an nur einer Wand wurde das Appartement derart aufgeteilt, dass Bereiche geschaffen wurden, die das Eindringen von Licht in andere Bereiche verhindern.

Dit appartement werd ontworpen voor een fotograaf die behoefte had aan ruimte om een deel van zijn werk te archiveren en op te slaan. De hoogte van het plafond maakte het mogelijk de ruimte maximaal te benutten. Door gebruik te maken van de ramen die allen in eenzelfde wand zitten, werd het appartement zodanig georganiseerd dat er ruimten gecreëerd werden die het licht naar andere sectoren leiden.

Este apartamento fue diseñado para un fotógrafo que quería espacio para organizar y guardar parte de su trabajo. La altura de los techos permitió un gran aprovechamiento del ambiente. Con las ventanas colocadas en una única pared, el apartamento se organizó de tal forma que se generan espacios que obstruyen el paso de la luz hacia otros sectores.

JOHN BARMAN

John Barman Residence

Located in the area known as Park Avenue's Crystal Corridor, the apartments in this building were designed using the original 1959 modernist structure that once housed offices. The remodeling process rationalized the interior architecture to create a modern and personal feel. The color scheme is characterized by contrasts between red and white, enhanced by large-scale art works.

Situés dans la zone connue sous le nom de Crystal Corridor de Park Avenue, les appartements de cet édifice s'érigent sur une structure moderniste construite en 1959, qui abrite des bureaux. Au cours du processus de rénovation, l'architecture intérieure a été rationalisée de manière à créer une pièce moderne et intime. La palette des couleurs est caractérisée par les contrastes entre le rouge et le blanc, le tout renforcé par les œuvres d'art grand format.

Situati nella zona nota come il Crystal Corridor di Park Avenue, gli appartamenti di questo edificio si ergono su una struttura modernista originale del 1959 che ospitava degli uffici. Durante la ristrutturazione sono stati razionalizzati gli spazi interni per creare un ambiente moderno e personale. La gamma di colori utilizzata si caratterizza per i contrasti tra rosso e bianco, rafforzati da opere d'arte di grandi dimensioni.

Die Appartements dieses Gebäudes in einem als Crystal Corridor von Park Avenue bekannten Gebiet, wurden auf einer ursprünglichen Jugendstilstruktur von 1959 für Büroräume erbaut. Beim Umbau wurde die Innenarchitektur rationalisiert, um ein modernes und persönliches Ambiente zu schaffen. Die Farbpalette kennzeichnet sich durch Kontraste zwischen rot und weiß und wird durch großformatige Kunstwerke noch weiter verstärkt.

De appartementen van dit gebouw, gelegen in de zone die bekendstaat als de Crystal Corridor van Park Avenue, werden opgetrokken op de oorspronkelijke modernistische structuur uit 1959 die destijds kantoren herbergde. In het verbouwingsproces werd de binnenhuisarchitectuur gerationaliseerd om een moderne en persoonlijke omgeving te creëren. Het kleurenpalet wordt gekenmerkt door de contrasten tussen rood en wit, versterkt door de grootschalige kunstwerken.

Estos apartamentos situados en la zona conocida como el Crystal Corridor de Park Avenue se construyeron aprovechando la estructura modernista del edificio original de 1959 que albergaba oficinas. En el proceso de remodelación se racionalizó la arquitectura interior para crear un ambiente moderno y personal. La paleta de colores se caracteriza por los contrastes entre el rojo y el blanco, reforzado por las obras de arte de gran formato.

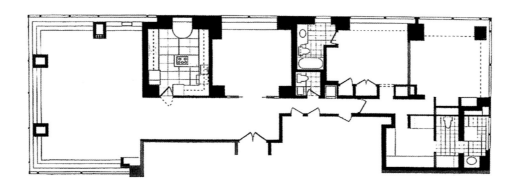

JOHN LEE, ALEX GIL, KARIN TEHVE/WORKSHOP FOR ARCHITECTURE

Swinehart Loft

The popular Tribeca district, with an abundance of lofts featuring elegant and clean lines, has become one of New York's most fashionable areas. Many lofts have been turned into art galleries, cafés, restaurants, and stores. This apartment reflects this trend with a clean and simple design that exposes part of the original structure and highlights the luxury details.

Le quartier populaire de Tribeca, qui regorge de lofts aux lignes élégantes et épurées, est devenu l'un des endroits les plus modernes de Manhattan. De nombreux lofts se sont transformés en galeries d'art, cafés, restaurants et boutiques. Cette habitation est le reflet de cette tendance, un appartement au design clair et simple qui, en laissant apparaître une partie de la structure d'origine, met en valeur les détails de luxe.

Il popolare quartiere di Tribeca, dove troviamo numerosi *loft* dalle linee pure ed eleganti, si è trasformato in una delle zone più moderne di Manhattan. Molti *loft* sono stati trasformati in gallerie d'arte, caffè, ristoranti e negozi. Questa casa riflette tale tendenza; si tratta di un appartamento dalle linee semplici e chiare che, mantenendo parte della struttura originale in vista, dà risalto ai dettagli di lusso.

Das berühmte Tribeca Viertel, in dem *Lofts* mit eleganten und reinen Linien vorherrschen, hat sich in eines der modernsten Gebiete Manhattans verwandelt. Viele *Lofts* wurden zu Kunstgalerien, Cafés, Restaurants und Geschäften. Ein Zeichen dieses Trends ist diese Wohnung. Es handelt sich um ein Appartement mit einem klaren und einfachen Entwurf. Ein sichtbarer Teil der Originalstruktur hebt die Luxusdetails hervor.

Het populaire Tribeca-district, waar het wemelt van de *lofts* met elegante en zuivere lijnen is één van de modernste zones van Manhattan geworden. Talrijke *lofts* werden omgevormd tot kunstgalerijen, cafés, restaurants en winkels. Deze woning weerspiegelt deze tendens helemaal. Het betreft een appartement met een helder en eenvoudig ontwerp dat de oorspronkelijke structuur gedeeltelijk zichtbaar laat en zo de luxedetails extra tot zijn recht laat komen.

El popular distrito de Tribeca, donde abundan los *lofts* de líneas elegantes y puras, se ha convertido en una de las áreas de moda de Manhattan. Muchos *lofts* se han convertido en galerías de arte, cafés, restaurantes y tiendas. Reflejo de esta tendencia es el caso de este apartamento, con un diseño claro y sencillo que deja parte de la estructura original a la vista y realza los detalles de lujo.

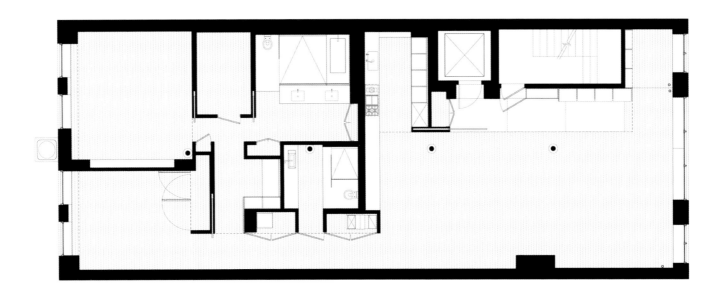

JORDAN MOZER & ASSOCIATES

Renaissance Hotel

The recently renovated Renaissance Hotel in Times Square looks amazing following the dazzling face lift entrusted to the experienced hands of Jordan Mozer. The 26 stories feature spectacular custom-made furniture, deeply luxurious bathrooms and salons, and restaurants that might have been created by a 21st-century Visconti. Of note is the clear distinction between styles seen in the different ambiances, giving the whole a certain museum-like air.

L'hôtel Renaissance de Times Square vient d'être rénové, et montre un nouveau visage éblouissant grâce à l'expérience de Jordan Mozer. Après son intervention, les 26 étages du complexe sont dotés d'un mobilier spectaculaire créé tout spécialement pour l'occasion, de salles de bains au luxe incomparable et de salons et de restaurants qui auraient aussi bien pu être l'œuvre d'un Visconti du XXIe siècle. Il faut remarquer la claire distinction entre les styles des différentes atmosphères, qui donne à l'ensemble une certaine qualité muséologique.

Rinnovato di recente, l'Hotel Renaissance, situato in Times Squame, attira l'attenzione per il suo magnifico restauro affidato all'esperienza di Jordan Mozer. Dopo l'intervento, i 26 piani del complesso vantano uno spettacolare arredamento creato ex profeso, bagni di un lusso senza paragoni, saloni e ristoranti che potrebbero essere stati creati da un Visconti del XXI secolo. Bisogna sottolineare poi la netta distinzione tra gli stili che si osserva nei vari ambienti, il che conferisce all'insieme una certa atmosfera da museo.

Erst kürzlich renoviert, beeindruckt das Renaissance Hotel am Times Square mit einem blendenden Facelifting, das dem erfahrenen Jordan Mozer anvertraut wurde. Die 26 Etagen des Komplexes sind nun mit spektakulärem Mobiliar ausgestattet, das eigens hierfür entworfen wurde. Sie verfügen über Badezimmer von unvergleichlichem Luxus sowie Salons und Restaurants, die von einem Visconti des 21. Jahrhunderts entworfen zu sein scheinen. Bleibt noch die klare Differenzierung der Stile hervorzuheben, die man in den unterschiedlichen Ambienten beobachtet; dies verleiht dem Ganzen einen gewissen musealen Anstrich.

Het onlangs gerenoveerde Renaissance Hotel op Times Square ziet er, dankzij de oogverblindende opknapbeurt van de ervaren Jordan Mozer, fantastisch uit. Na de ingreep, beroemen de 26 verdiepingen van het complex zich op spectaculair op maat gemaakt meubilair, ongelooflijk luxueuze badkamers, zalen en restaurants die door een Visconti van de XXIe eeuw gecreëerd hadden kunnen zijn. Het is belangrijk de aandacht te vestigen op de verschillende stijlen die aan het geheel een museumachtig karakter verleent.

Recién renovado, el Hotel Renaissance situado en Times Square impresiona con el deslumbrante lavado de cara confiado a la experiencia de Jordan Mozer. Tras la intervención, las 26 plantas del complejo presumen de un espectacular mobiliario creado ex profeso, cuartos de baño de lujo incomparable, y salones y restaurantes que podrían haber sido creados por un Visconti del siglo XXI. Cabe destacar la clara distinción entre estilos que se observa en los distintos ambientes, lo cual dota al conjunto de cierto aire museístico.

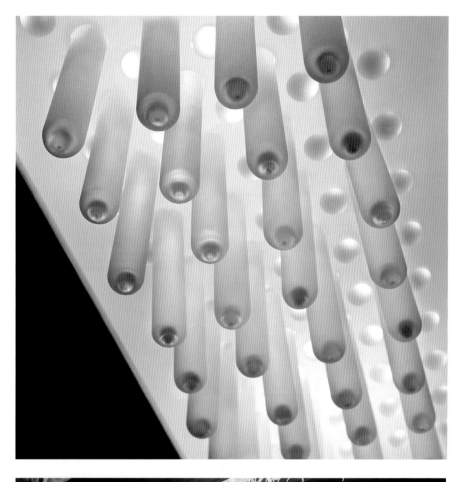

KARIM RASHID

Loft by Karim Rashid

Designed as a single space, this loft has no other partitions other than those strictly required to define the only two rooms: bedroom and bathroom. The remaining space is open, and features bright colors, sensations of volume and texture, and the constant search for new combinations.

Pensé comme espace unique, ce loft ne dispose que de très peu de cloisons, celles-ci se limitant à définir les deux seules pièces de l'habitation : la chambre et la salle de bain. Le reste a été conçu comme un espace ouvert soulignant les couleurs chatoyantes, les sensations de volume et de textures, et la recherche constante de nouvelles combinaisons.

Progettato come spazio unico, questo *loft* non ha pareti tranne quelle strettamente necessarie a definire le due uniche stanze esistenti: camera e bagno. Il resto è stato concepito come uno spazio aperto in cui si impongono vivaci colori, sensazioni di volumi e consistenze, oltre alla ricerca costante di nuove combinazioni.

Dieses *Loft* wurde als einheitlicher Bereich entworfen und besitzt keine weiteren Wände als die für die beiden einzigen vorhandenen Räume, d. h. für Schlafzimmer und Bad, streng erforderlichen Wände. Der Rest wurde als offener Raum gestaltet, in dem sich knallige Farben, Eindrücke der Volumen und Texturen, sowie die konstante Suche nach neuen Kombinationen, hervorheben.

In deze *loft*, gepland als één enkele ruimte, werden slechts de wanden aangebracht die strikt noodzakelijk zijn om de twee enige bestaande vertrekken af te bakenen: de slaapkamer en de badkamer. De rest werd ontworpen als een open ruimte waar opvallende kleuren, de sensaties van volumes en texturen en de voortdurende zoektocht naar nieuwe combinaties overheersen.

Proyectado como espacio único, este *loft* carece de paredes más allá de las estrictamente necesarias para definir las dos únicas habitaciones existentes: el dormitorio y el baño. El resto se ha concebido como un espacio abierto donde destacan los colores llamativos, las sensaciones de volumen y texturas, y la búsqueda constante de nuevas combinaciones.

KAZUYO SEJIMA & RYUE NISHIZAWA/SANAA

New Museum of Contemporary Art

The first floor of this new cultural site houses a large lobby, coffee shop and a gift and curios store. There are four public galleries in the building and a further three exhibition spaces for temporary shows, located in open, column-free spaces. All the galleries have skylights on the ceilings, giving the interiors the privilege of natural lighting. The basement houses an assembly room and a large storage space.

Le rez-de-chaussée de ce nouvel établissement culturel abrite un grand vestibule, une cafétéria et une boutique de cadeaux et curiosités. Le bâtiment comprend quatre galeries publiques et trois autres espaces d'exposition temporaire dans des espaces ouverts sans colonnes. Toutes les galeries sont dotées de puits de lumière au plafond, ce qui donne aux espaces intérieurs le privilège d'un éclairage naturel. Une salle polyvalente et un grand espace de stockage ont été aménagés au sous-sol.

Il pianterreno di questa nuova sede culturale ospita un ampio vestibolo, una caffetteria e un negozio di regali e curiosità. Nell'edificio ci sono quattro gallerie pubbliche e altri tre spazi espositivi per mostre occasionali, in ambienti aperti senza colonne. Tutte le gallerie sono provviste di lucernari nel soffitto, che conferiscono agli interni il privilegio di un'illuminazione naturale. Nella cantina è stata abilitata una sala per conferenze e un grande spazio adibito a magazzino.

Das Erdgeschoss dieses neuen Kultursitzes umfasst eine großzügige Eingangshalle, Cafeterla, Geschenke- und Andenkenladen. Im Gebäude befinden sich vier öffentliche Galerien und weitere drei Bereiche für temporäre Austellungen, die in großzügigen Räumen ohne Säulen angesiedelt sind. Die Lichtkuppeln in der Decke aller Galerien verleihen dem Innenbereich eine Tageslichtbeleuchtung. Im Untergeschoss befinden sich ein Veranstaltungssaal und ein großer Lagerraum.

De benedenverdieping van dit nieuw cultureel centrum herbergt een ruime foyer, een lunchroom en een geschenken- en curiosawinkel. Het gebouw omvat, in een reeks open zuilenvrije ruimten, vier openbare galerijen en drie expositieruimten voor tijdelijke tentoonstellingen. In het dak van de galerijen zitten dakramen, waardoor de interieurs van natuurlijk licht genieten. In de kelder werd een aula en een grote opslagplaats ingericht.

La planta baja de esta nueva sede cultural comprende un amplio vestíbulo, una cafetería, y una tienda de regalos y curiosidades. Hay en el edificio cuatro galerías públicas y tres salas de exposición para muestras puntuales, ubicadas en espacios abiertos libres de columnas. Todas las galerías tienen lucernarios en el techo, otorgando a los interiores el privilegio de una iluminación natural. En el sótano hay habilitado un salón de actos y un gran espacio para almacenaje.

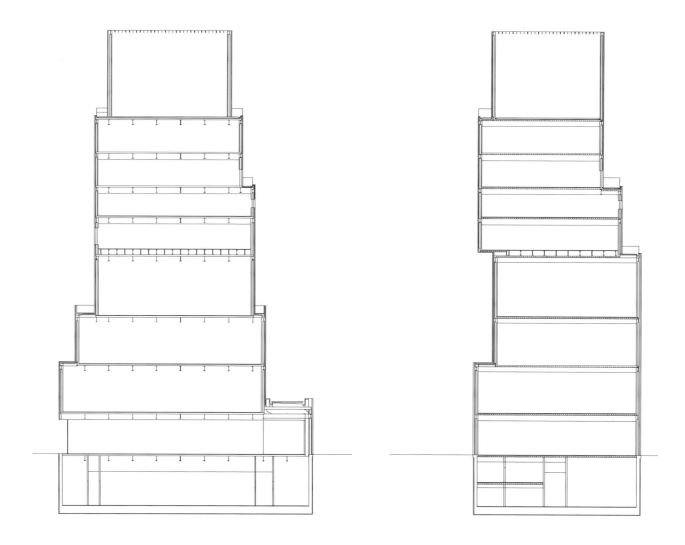

LEWIS.TSURUMAKI.LEWIS/LTL ARCHITECTS

Geltner Parker Loft

The commission consisted of renovating a loft in the southern part of Manhattan. Budget restrictions led the architect and clients to remodel only a part of the home and apply their efforts and money in stages. They did not try to blend the old with the new; instead the results of the remodeling were left open to view. The only unifying element acting is the staircase.

La commande consistait à rénover un loft au sud de Manhattan. Le budget disponible étant limité, les architectes et les clients ont décidé de ne réhabiliter qu'une seule partie du logement et de consacrer leurs efforts et leur argent pièce après pièce. Ils n'ont pas cherché l'unification entre l'ancien et le neuf, mais ont plutôt fait ressortir clairement la rénovation. L'unique élément servant de fil conducteur est l'escalier.

L'incarico prevedeva la ristrutturazione di un loft nel sud di Manhattan. A causa delle risorse economiche limitate, architetti e clienti hanno deciso di rinnovare solo una parte della struttura e distribuire energie e denaro in diverse fasi. Non si è cercato di unificare vecchio e nuovo, ma anzi si è dato risalto alla parte ristrutturata in modo evidente. L'unico elemento che funge da filo conduttore è la scala.

Der Auftrag lautete, ein Loft im Süden Manhattans zu renovieren. Aufgrund der begrenzten Mittel beschlossen Architekten und Auftraggeber, nur einen Teil der Wohnung zu renovieren und Arbeit und Geld phasenweise zu konzentrieren. Hierbei wurde keine Vereinigung zwischen Bestehendem und Neuem gesucht, sondern die Reform sichtbar hervorgehoben. Das einzige verbindungsschaffende Element ist die Treppe.

De opdracht bestond erin een loft ten zuiden van Manhattan te renoveren. Vanwege het beperkte budget, besloten architecten en klanten slechts één deel van de woning te restaureren en hun inspanningen en het geld fase per fase te investeren. Het doel was niet het bestaande en het nieuwe te unificeren, maar de verbouwing extra in de verf te zetten. Het enige element dat dienst doet als leidraad is de trap.

El encargo consistía en renovar un loft al sur de Manhattan. Debido a las limitaciones de presupuesto, arquitectos y clientes decidieron rehabilitar sólo una parte de la vivienda y concentrar esfuerzos y dinero por etapas. No se buscó la unificación entre lo existente y lo nuevo, sino que se resaltó la reforma de manera evidente. El único elemento que actúa de hilo conductor es la escalera.

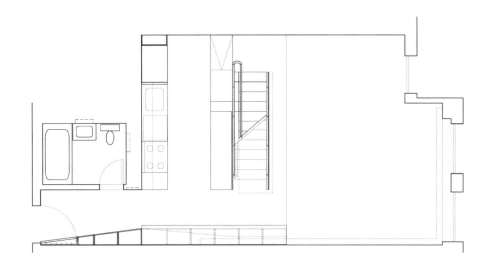

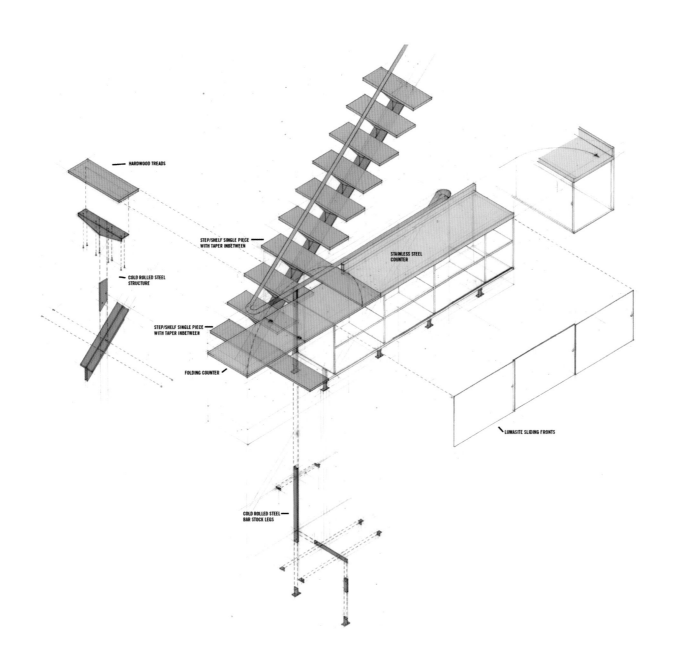

HARDWOOD TREADS

STEP/SHELF SINGLE PIECE
WITH TAPER INBETWEEN

STAINLESS STEEL
COUNTER

COLD ROLLED STEEL
STRUCTURE

STEP/SHELF SINGLE PIECE
WITH TAPER INBETWEEN

FOLDING COUNTER

LUMASITE SLIDING FRONTS

COLD ROLLED STEEL
BAR STOCK LEGS

LEWIS.TSURUMAKI.LEWIS/LTL ARCHITECTS

Xing Restaurant

The floor of this Chinese restaurant, housed in a typical NY tenement building, forms a bottleneck in the middle. Instead of trying to dissimulate this aspect, the architect opted to accentuate and make the most of it so that the interior design of the front half of the restaurant is completely different to the back. This enabled the creation of different ambiances through the use of diverse materials such as stone and bamboo for the more public areas and plush velvet upholstery for the private spaces.

Ce restaurant chinois présente un étranglement en son milieu, une caractéristique courante dans cette ville. Au lieu de dissimuler cet aspect, l'architecte a décidé de l'accentuer et d'en tirer parti. Il définit la limite entre deux décorations complètement différentes. Cela a permis de créer des ambiances qui se différencient grâce à leurs matériaux, comme la pierre et le bambou pour les espaces les plus publics, et une tapisserie de velours pour les espaces plus intimes.

La pianta di questo ristorante cinese (tipica di molti locali della città) delinea un collo di bottiglia nel suo stesso centro. Invece di cercare di nascondere questo elemento, l'architetto ha deciso di accentuarlo e utilizzarlo, in modo tale che, prima di arrivarvi, il design d'interni è completamente distinto da quello che lo segue. Grazie a ciò è stato possibile creare diversi ambienti, mediante l'utilizzo di materiali differenti, come la pietra e il bambù per le zone più pubbliche e la tappezzeria di velluto per gli spazi più raccolti.

Der Grundriss dieses Chinarestaurants in einem für New York typischen Mietshaus hat eine Engstelle in der Mitte. Anstatt diesen Aspekt zu verschleiern, entschied sich der Architekt dafür, ihn zu betonen und Nutzen daraus zu ziehen, was dazu führte, dass die Innengestaltung vor und hinter diesem Punkt sehr unterschiedlich ausfiel. Durch die Verwendung verschiedener Materialien, wie Stein und Bambus in den Bereichen mit mehr Publikumsverkehr und Samtbezügen in den intimeren Räumen, entstand ein jeweils anderes Ambiente.

De etage van dit Chinese restaurant, in een typisch New Yorks huurgebouw, wordt in het midden verdeeld door een versmalling dat een flessenhalseffect produceert. In plaats van dit aspect te willen verdoezelen, koos de architect ervoor het te benadrukken en voor en na twee totaal verschillende interieurs te ontwerpen. Hierdoor konden door het gebruik van diverse materialen verschillende ruimten gecreëerd worden: steen en bamboe voor de meer publieke zones en fluwelen bekledingen voor de intiemere zones.

La planta de este restaurante chino –típica en la ciudad– presenta un estrechamiento en el centro. En lugar de tratar de disimular este aspecto, el arquitecto decidió acentuarlo y sacarle partido, de manera que los diseños de las partes delantera y trasera son completamente distintos. Esto permitió la creación de distintos ambientes mediante el empleo de materiales diversos, como la piedra y el bambú para las zonas más públicas y el tapizado de terciopelo para los espacios más recogidos.

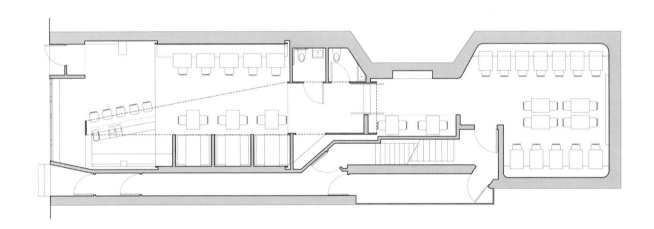

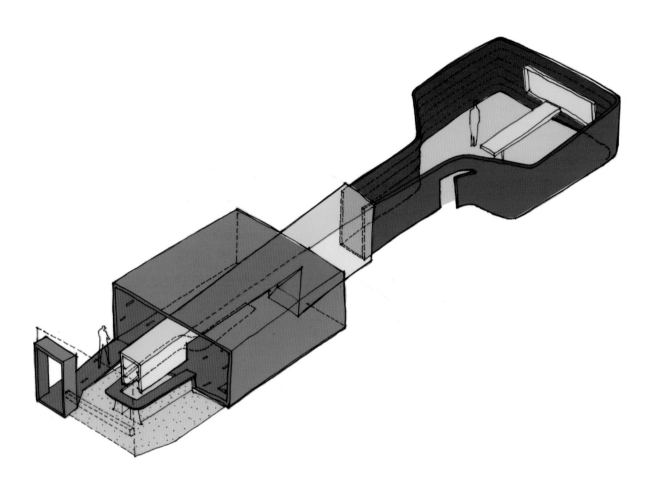

MICHAEL OVERINGTON & ANDA ANDREI/IAN SCHRAGER

Gramercy Park Hotel

This legendary hotel, built in 1924 and favored throughout the 20th century by figures like the Kennedys, Humphrey Bogart and Babe Ruth, was spectacularly renovated by the collaborators of proprietor Ian Schrager, who in turn received the inestimable aid of the painter Julian Schnabel. With its classic look and theatrical decor, the hotel now features an ambiance loaded with elements reminiscent of the work of Philippe Starck. The predominance of red tones and satin fabrics is striking and welcoming at once.

Cet hôtel légendaire a été construit en 1924 et a été fréquenté tout au long du XXᵉ siècle par des personnages tels que la famille Kennedy, Humphrey Bogart ou Babe Ruth. Les collaborateurs du propriétaire, Ian Schrager, lui ont fait subir une rénovation spectaculaire, pour laquelle ils ont pu compter sur l'aide inestimable du peintre Julian Schnabel. L'atmosphère de cet établissement classique, dont la décoration évoque un théâtre, est à présent chargée de réminiscences du travail de Philippe Starck. La prédominance du rouge et des tissus satinés donne un résultat grandiose mais convivial.

Questo leggendario hotel, costruito nel 1924 e frequentato nel XX secolo da personalità come i Kennedy, Humphrey Bogart e Babe Ruth, è stato sottoposto a una spettacolare riforma dai collaboratori del proprietario, Ian Schrager, i quali a loro volta hanno ricevuto un aiuto inestimabile da parte del pittore Julian Schnabel. Caratterizzato da un aspetto classico e una decorazione teatrale, l'hotel mostra ora un ambiente molto carico, con reminiscenze del lavoro di Philippe Starck. Il predominio di tonalità rosse e tele satin offre una sensazione di forte impatto, pur risultando accogliente.

Dieses legendäre Hotel, 1924 errichtet und im vergangenen Jahrhundert von Persönlichkeiten wie den Kennedys, Humphrey Bogart und Babe Ruth vorzugsweise frequentiert, wurde auf spektakuläre Weise von den Mitarbeitern des Eigentümers Ian Schrager saniert, welche ihrerseits auf die unschätzbare Unterstützung des Malers Julian Schnabel bauen durften. Von klassischem Aussehen und mit einer Dekoration, die an die Welt des Theaters erinnert, zeigt das Hotel nun ein Ambiente voller Reminiszenzen des Philippe Starck-Designs. Das Vorherrschen roter Töne und glänzender Stoffe wirkt beeindruckend und gleichzeitig gemütlich.

Dit legendarische hotel, gebouwd in 1924 en doorheen de XXe eeuw de favoriete plek van figuren als de Kennedy's, Humphrey Bogart en Babe Ruth, werd op spectaculaire wijze gerenoveerd door de medewerkers van de eigenaar, Ian Schrager, die op hun beurt mochten rekenen op de onschatbare hulp van de schilder Julian Schnabel. Het hotel dat er klassiek uitziet met theatrale toetsen, baadt nu in een sfeer die beladen is met herinneringen aan het werk van Philippe Starck. De overheersende rode tonen en gesatineerde stoffen leiden tot een overweldigend en tegelijkertijd gezellig resultaat.

Este legendario hotel, construido en 1924 y preferido a lo largo del siglo XX por figuras como los Kennedy, Humphrey Bogart y Babe Ruth, fue espectacularmente renovado por los colaboradores del propietario, Ian Schrager, que a su vez contaron con la ayuda inestimable del pintor Julian Schnabel. De aspecto clásico y decoración de evocaciones teatrales, el hotel muestra ahora un ambiente recargado con reminiscencias del trabajo de Philippe Starck. El predominio de tonos rojos y telas satinadas resulta impactante a la vez que acogedor.

nARCHITECTS

Switch Building

This striking seven-storey building on the Lower East Side houses four apartments that cover a floor each, a two-storey penthouse and an art gallery located on the ground floor and in the basement. The play of the angular facade which rises and falls on each alternate floor gives all the occupants fantastic views over Norfolk Street and also creates an interesting effect of shadows and reflections. At the rear of each apartment, the living room extends into spacious balconies which are also alternated to run along different sides of the floor, depending on their height within the building.

Cet immeuble étonnant situé dans le Lower East Side abrite quatre appartements qui occupent chacun un étage entier, un attique de deux étages et une galerie d'art sur deux hauteurs, au rez-de-chaussée et au sous-sol. Le jeu de la façade angulaire, dont chaque étage forme une saillie d'un côté et de l'autre alternativement, permet de donner aux occupants de chaque étage les meilleures vues sur la rue Norfolk, et crée en même temps un effet d'ombres et de reflets intéressant. Dans la partie arrière de chaque appartement, le salon est prolongé par de grands balcons qui eux aussi s'étendent en alternance de différents côtés de l'édifice selon l'étage auquel ils appartiennent.

Questo vistoso edificio di sette piani del Lower East Side ospita quattro appartamenti che occupano ognuno un piano intero, un attico di due piani e una galleria d'arte su due livelli, situata al pianterreno e nelle cantine. Il gioco creato dalla facciata angolare, che forma picchi alternati in base al piano, offre agli occupanti di ogni piano le migliori viste sulla Norfolk Street e, nello stesso tempo, crea un interessante effetto di ombre e riflessi. Nella parte posteriore di ogni appartamento, il soggiorno si apre su ampi balconi, che si alternano e si allungano anch'essi in vari lati del piano, secondo l'altezza che occupano nell'edificio.

Das auffällige siebenstöckige Gebäude an der Lower East Side umfasst vier Apartments, die sich über jeweils eine Etage erstrecken, eine zweistöckige Penthouse-Wohnung und eine Kunstgalerie, die auf zwei Ebenen angelegt ist und sich im Erdgeschoss bzw. Souterrain befindet. Das Spiel der je nach Stockwerk abwechselnd auskragenden Winkel an der Fassade erlaubt es, den Bewohnern in jeder Etage die besten Ausblicke auf die Norfolk Street zu gewähren. Gleichzeitig entsteht ein interessanter Effekt durch die Schatten und Reflexe. Auf der Rückseite der Apartments läuft das Wohnzimmer jeweils zu einem großzügigen Balkon hin aus. Auch diese Balkone springen abhängig von der Höhe des Stockwerks an unterschiedlichen Stellen des Gebäudes hervor.

Dit opvallende gebouw met zeven verdiepingen op het Lower East Side herbergt vier appartementen van een volledige etage, een penthouse van tweehoog en een kunstgalerij op de benedenverdieping en in de kelder. Het spel dat gecreëerd wordt door de hoekige gevel met wisselende uitsteeksels over de diverse verdiepingen, geeft de bewoners uitstekend uitzicht op Norfolk Street en zorgt voor een interessant effect van schaduwen en reflecties. Aan de achterkant van elk appartement loopt de zitkamer uit op ruime balkons die ook afgewisseld worden aan weerszijden van elke etage naargelang de plaats die ze in het gebouw inneemt.

Este llamativo edificio de siete plantas del Lower East Side alberga cuatro apartamentos de planta entera, un ático de dos pisos y una galería de arte de dos alturas, situada en la planta baja y en los sótanos. El juego de la fachada angular, donde las plantas forman un saliente en un lado y otro alternativamente, permite brindar a los ocupantes de cada piso las mejores vistas de la calle Norfolk, y a la vez crea un interesante efecto de sombras y reflejos. En la parte trasera de cada apartamento, el salón se extiende en amplios balcones, que también se alternan y alargan en lados distintos de la planta, dependiendo de la altura que ocupan en el edificio.

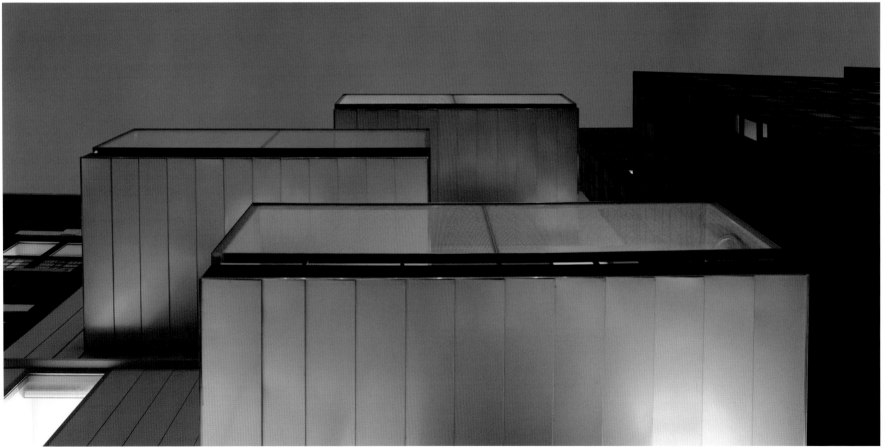

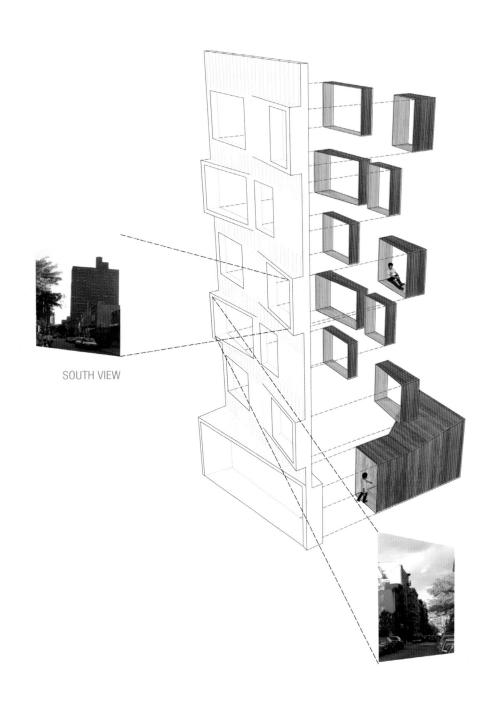

SOUTH VIEW

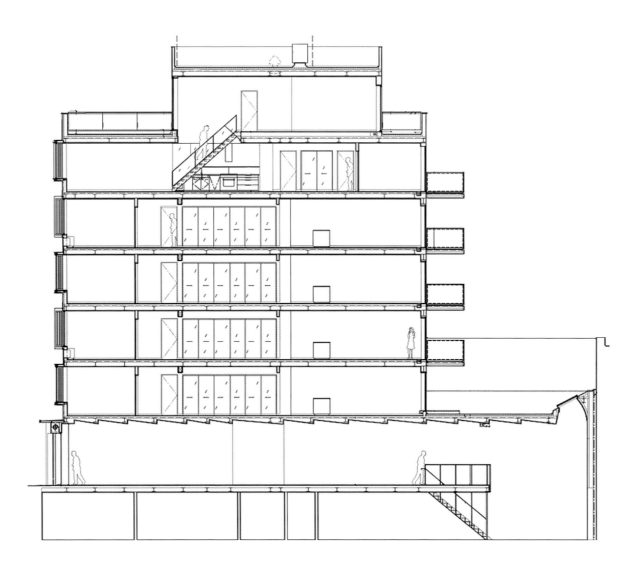

RENZO PIANO BUILDING WORKSHOP

The New York Times Building

The new head offices of one of the world's most important newspapers is a 52-storey building that is almost transparent and very permeable for the circulation of its occupants. For the façade, instead of the mirrored surfaces that are so fashionable, the architect opted for clear, translucent glass which turns blue when it rains and red at sunset. A very open vestibule and a large indoor garden free to the public speak to a public-service vocation in tune with a newspaper's work of keeping the public informed.

Le nouveau siège de l'un des plus grands journaux du monde est un immeuble de 52 étages presque transparent et très perméable à la circulation de ses occupants. On remarque sur sa façade, au lieu des surfaces miroir si prisées habituellement, du verre clair et translucide qui prend des teintes bleues après la pluie et rouges au coucher du soleil. Le vestibule très ouvert et le grand jardin intérieur sont ouverts à tous, en harmonie avec la vocation de service public associée au travail d'information journalistique.

La nuova sede di uno dei giornali più importanti del mondo è un edificio di 52 piani quasi trasparente e molto permeabile alla circolazione dei suoi occupanti. Sulla facciata, invece delle superfici a specchio tanto di moda, è stato posto un vetro chiaro e semitrasparente, che diventa azzurrognolo, dopo una pioggia, e rossiccio, con il tramonto. E' possibile accedere liberamente a un vestibolo molto aperto e a un ampio giardino interno, il che dimostra una vocazione di servizio pubblico che si sposa con il lavoro informativo di un giornale.

Der neue Sitz einer der wichtigsten Zeitungen der Welt ist ein fast transparentes 52-stöckiges Gebäude, das günstig für die interne Bewegungsfreiheit der Angestellten ist. Für die Fassade wurde anstelle der modischen Spiegeloberflächen helles und lichtdurchlässiges Glas verwendet, das nach Regen bläulich und bei Sonneneinstrahlung rötlich wirkt. Eine weit offene Vorhalle und ein weitläufiger Innengarten sind frei für jeden frei zugänglich. Das korrespondiert mit der Funktion des Gebäudes, das als Medienanstalt im Dienste der Öffentlichkeit steht.

De nieuwe hoofdzetel van één van de belangrijkste kranten ter wereld is een gebouw met 52 verdiepingen dat bijna geheel doorzichtig is en waarin de mensen heel gemakkelijk kunnen circuleren. In plaats van trendy spiegeloppervlakken, koos de architect voor een gevel met helder, doorzichtig glas, dat een blauwe schijn aanneemt wanneer het regent, en een roodachtige bij zonsondergang. Een zeer open foyer en een ruime binnentuin die vrij toegankelijk is voor het publiek verwijst naar de roeping van de krant: dienstverlening en publieksinformatie.

La nueva sede de uno de los periódicos más importantes del mundo es un edificio de 52 plantas casi transparente, muy permeable a la circulación de sus ocupantes. De su fachada, en lugar de las superficies-espejo tan en boga, destaca el cristal claro y translúcido, que se torna azulado tras la lluvia y rojizo con la puesta de sol. Un vestíbulo muy abierto y un amplio jardín interior son de libre acceso, redundando en una vocación de servicio público que casa con la labor informativa de un periódico.

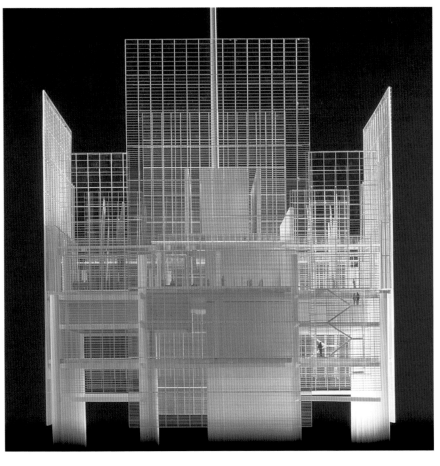
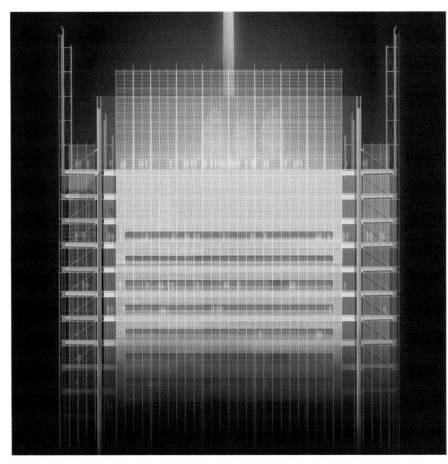

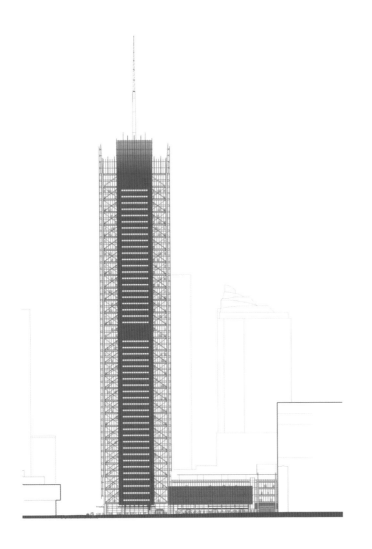

RESOLUTION: 4 ARCHITECTURE

Eisenman Davidson

Designed for the architect Peter Eisenman and his family, this apartment combines three units to create a residential space that is highly adapted to the needs of the people living in it. Art works and books become as important to the home as its design, the purpose of which was to provide space for the large and varied collection accumulated from the owners' experiences and travels.

Conçu pour l'architecte Peter Eisenman et sa famille, cet appartement allie trois unités pour créer un espace résidentiel hautement adapté aux nécessités de ses occupants. Les œuvres d'art et les livres deviennent une partie de l'habitation aussi importante que son design, qui doit réserver un espace pour la collection vaste et variée complétée au fil de l'expérience et des voyages des propriétaires.

Progettato per l'architetto Peter Eisenman e la sua famiglia, questo appartamento combina insieme tre unità per creare uno spazio residenziale fortemente adattato alle necessità dei suoi abitanti. Le opere d'arte e i libri si trasformano in una parte importante della casa così come il suo design, con l'obiettivo di creare lo spazio necessario alla vasta e varia collezione, frutto dell'esperienza e dei viaggi dei proprietari della casa.

Dieses Appartement wurde für den Architekten Peter Eisenman und seine Familie entworfen und verbindet drei Einheiten, um einen Wohnbereich zu schaffen, der den Bedürfnissen seiner Bewohner genau angepasst ist. Kunstwerke und Bücher erhalten im Haus die gleiche Bedeutung wie sein Design, um Raum für die große und vielgestaltige Sammlung aus Erfahrungen und Reisen der Hausbesitzer zu schaffen.

Dit appartement, ontworpen voor de architect Peter Eisenman en zijn familie, combineert drie units om een residentiële ruimte te creëren die in hoge mate aangepast is aan de behoeften van de bewoners. De kunstwerken en boeken werden een even belangrijk onderdeel van het huis als het ontwerp zelf, met als doel een ruimte te voorzien voor de uitgebreide en gevarieerde collectie die voortkomt uit de ervaring en reizen van de eigenaars van het huis.

Diseñado para el arquitecto Peter Eisenman y su familia, este apartamento combina tres unidades para crear un espacio residencial altamente adaptado a las necesidades de sus habitantes. Las obras de arte y los libros se convierten en una parte tan importante de la casa como su diseño, con el objeto de proporcionar espacio para la amplia y variada colección resultante de la experiencia y los viajes de los dueños de la casa.

O. M. UNGERS

An Exhibition of Architecture, May 6 to May 31, 1977

The Institute for Architecture and Urban Studies
8 West 40th Street, New York, NY 10018

ROB KRIER

An Exhibition of Drawings, April 18 to May 2, 1977

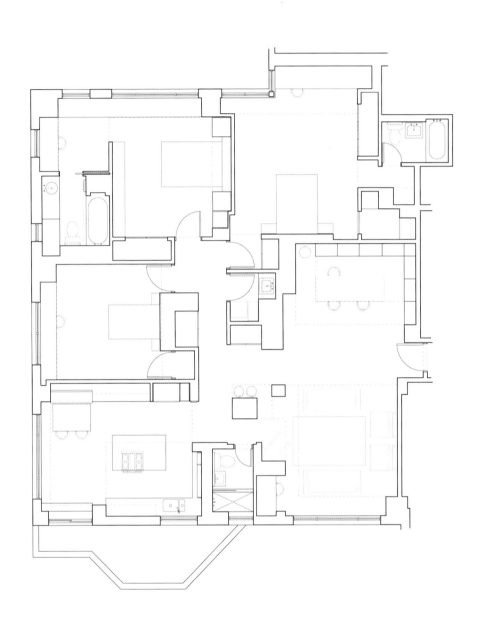

RESOLUTION: 4 ARCHITECTURE

Nychay Loft

Located in a new building of loft-style homes in central New York, this project was designed for a young professional as an urban base. The project involved addressing the duality that exists between creating an open-plan space and protecting privacy. The result is a contrast between the sophistication of a high-quality contemporary residential project and the primitive appeal of an industrial building in the historic Soho district.

Situé dans un nouvel édifice de lofts au cœur de New York, le projet a été conçu par un jeune professionnel comme son enclave urbaine. Le travail a essayé de flirter avec la dualité existante entre un espace ouvert et le respect de l'intimité. Le résultat obtenu est un contraste entre le caractère sophistiqué d'un projet résidentiel contemporain de haute qualité et le caractère primitif d'un édifice industriel situé dans le quartier historique de Soho.

Situato in un nuovo edificio di *loft* nel centro di New York, il progetto è stato pensato per un giovane professionista come la sua enclave urbana. Il lavoro ha cercato di esprimere la dualità esistente tra uno spazio aperto e il rispetto dell'intimità. Il risultato è un contrasto tra sofisticazione di un progetto contemporaneo di alta qualità residenziale e il primitivismo di un edificio industriale nello storico quartiere di Soho.

Das in einem neuen *Loft* - Gebäude im Zentrum vom New York gelegene Projekt wurde für einen jungen Freiberufler als einziger städtischer Raum geschaffen. Bei der Arbeit wurde versucht, die zwischen offenem Raum und Intimsphäre bestehende Dualität zu lösen. Das Ergebnis ist ein Kontrast zwischen Verfeinerung eines zeitgenössischen Projekts hoher Wohnqualität und der Primitivität eines Industriegebäudes im historischen Stadtteil Soho.

Het project, gelegen in een nieuw *loftgebouw* in het centrum van New York, werd ontworpen voor een jonge zelfstandige als zijn enige stadsenclave. Het werk streefde ernaar de bestaande dualiteit tussen een open ruimte en het behoud van de intimiteit aan te pakken. Het resultaat is een contrast tussen het raffinement van een hedendaags project met een hoge residentiële waarde en het primitivisme van een industrieel gebouw in de historische Soho-buurt.

Situado en un nuevo edificio de *lofts* en el centro de Nueva York, el proyecto fue diseñado para un joven profesional como su enclave urbano. El trabajo trató de abordar la dualidad existente entre un espacio abierto y el resguardo de la intimidad. El resultado es un contraste entre la sofisticación de un proyecto contemporáneo de alta calidad residencial y el primitivismo de un edificio industrial en el histórico barrio del Soho.

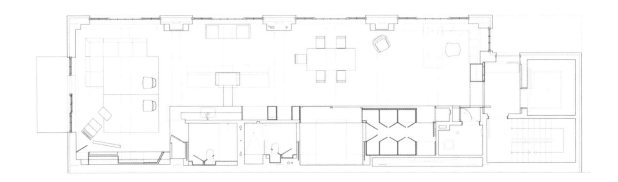

Coulter Apartment

The reorganization of this residence involved reducing the number of bedrooms from 3 to 2, opening up the common areas and making room for the impressive modern art collection belonging to the owner. With this in mind, the living room walls were knocked down and the ceilings raised while the floor was covered in white walnut. A bronze and glass wall separates the dining room from the study. Several mirrors were positioned to make the different views from various angles more accessible.

La reconversion de cette résidence avait pour objectif de réduire le nombre de chambres de 3 à 2, d'ouvrir les espaces communs et d'aménager des espaces pour l'impressionnante collection d'art contemporain du propriétaire. Les cloisons du salon ont donc été abattues, la hauteur des plafonds a été augmentée, et les sols ont été recouverts de bois de Nogal blanc. Un mur de bronze et de verre sépare la salle à manger du studio. Plusieurs miroirs ont également été installés afin de faciliter l'accès aux différentes vues panoramiques depuis différents angles des lieux.

La riorganizzazione di questa abitazione intendeva ridurre il numero di camere da 3 a 2, aprire gli spazi comuni e abilitare spazi vuoti per l'impressionante collezione d'arte moderna del proprietario. Con questo fine, sono state abbattute le pareti divisorie del soggiorno si è aumentata l'altezza dei soffitti, mentre i pavimenti sono stati coperti di legno di noce bianco. Un muro di bronzo e cristallo separa la sala da pranzo dallo studio. Inoltre, sono stati collocati vari specchi per moltiplicare le varie panoramiche visibili da diversi punti dell'appartamento.

Die Umstrukturierung dieser Wohnresidenz zog es nach sich, dass die Anzahl der Schlafzimmer von drei auf zwei reduziert, die Gemeinschaftsräume geöffnet und der so gewonnene Raum für die Präsentation der eindrucksvollen Sammlung moderner Kunst des Eigentümers hergerichtet wurde. Zu diesem Zweck riss man die Trennwände des Salons ein und erhöhte die Decken, während man die Fußböden mit weißem Nussbaumholz auslegte. Eine Wand aus Bronze und Glas trennt das Esszimmer vom Arbeitsstudio. Außerdem brachte man mehrere Spiegel an, um Ausblicke aus unterschiedlichen Blickwinkeln der Etage leichter zugänglich zu machen.

Voor de herstructurering van deze woning moest het aantal slaapkamers van 3 op 2 teruggebracht worden en diende er in de gemeenschappelijke zones plaats vrijgemaakt te worden om plaats te maken voor de indrukwekkende collectie moderne kunst van de eigenaar. Met dit doel voor ogen werden in de zitkamer tussenschotten weggehaald en werden de plafonds opgetrokken, terwijl de vloeren bekleed werden met wit notenhout. Een wand uit brons en glas scheidt de eetkamer van de studeerkamer. Er werden ook verscheidene spiegels aangebracht om vanuit verschillende hoeken een beter overzicht te krijgen van de etage.

La reconversión de esta residencia acarreaba reducir el número de dormitorios de 3 a 2, abrir los espacios comunes y habilitar huecos para la impresionante colección de arte moderno del propietario. Con este fin, se derribaron los tabiques del salón y se elevó la altura de los techos, mientras que los suelos fueron cubiertos con madera de nogal blanco. Un muro de bronce y cristal separa el comedor del estudio. Asimismo, se colocaron varios espejos para hacer más accesibles las distintas panorámicas desde distintos ángulos de la planta.

SKIDMORE, OWINGS & MERRILL

7 World Trade Center

This newly built block marks the start of the renovated space of the World Trade Center and exemplifies the spirit of new development of lower Manhattan. With a total of 52 floors, including 42 for offices and 10 that house services plus an electricity substation, it has been lined with floor-to-ceiling glass sheets on each floor and is illuminated at night via a complex LED system of sequential projections.

Ce bâtiment de construction récente marque l'entrée du nouvel espace du World Trade Center et représente l'esprit du nouveau développement de la partie basse de Manhattan. Avec un total de 52 étages (42 de bureaux en location et 10 qui accueillent les services et une sous-station électrique), l'immeuble est revêtu de panneaux de verre qui vont du sol au plafond de chaque étage, et qui sont éclairés de nuit par un système complexe de LED doté de séquence de projections.

Questo edificio di nuova costruzione costituisce l'accesso al rinnovato spazio del World Trade Center ed esemplifica lo spirito del nuovo sviluppo della bassa Manhattan. Con un totale di 52 piani (42 destinati all'affitto di uffici e dieci che ospitano tanto i servizi quanto una sottostazione elettrica), l'immobile è rivestito di pannelli di vetro che vanno dal pavimento al soffitto di ogni piano, illuminati di notte con un complesso sistema LED con proiezioni in sequenza.

Der Neubau markiert den Beginn für das erneuerte Areal des World Trade Centers und steht für den Geist einer aktuellen Entwicklung in Lower Manhattan. Das Bauwerk umfasst insgesamt 52 Stockwerke — davon stehen 42 für Büros zur Anmietung zur Verfügung, zehn für die Haustechnik und andere Dienste wie auch für ein elektrisches Umspannungswerk. Das Gebäude ist mit Glasscheiben verkleidet, die jeweils vom Boden bis zur Decke eines jeden Stockwerks reichen und nachts mit einem komplexen LED-System erleuchtet werden, das eine Folge von Lichtprojektionen zeigt.

Deze nieuwbouw is de eerste renovatiestap van de ruimte rondom het verdwenen World Trade Center en staat voor de nieuwe ontwikkelingssfeer van laag Manhattan. Elke verdieping van het gebouw, met een totaal van 52 verdiepingen —42 voor kantoren en tien voor diensten waaronder een elektriciteitsstation-, werd van onder tot boven bekleed met glazen panelen die 's nachts verlicht worden door een complex ledsysteem dat een reeks projecties vertoont.

Este edificio de nueva construcción marca el acceso al renovado espacio del World Trade Center y ejemplifica el espíritu de nuevo desarrollo del bajo Manhattan. Con un total de 52 plantas –42 para alquiler de oficinas y 10 que albergan tanto los servicios como una subestación eléctrica–, el inmueble viene forrado con paneles de cristal que van del suelo al techo de cada planta, iluminados de noche con un complejo sistema LED con secuencia de proyecciones.

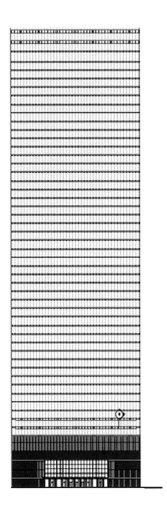

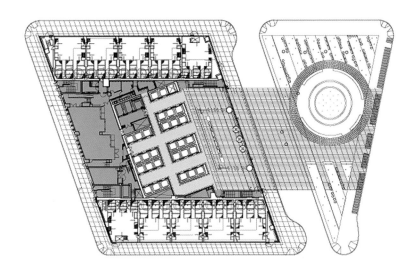

SKIDMORE, OWINGS & MERRILL

Tribeca Building

This multi-function mixed-use skyscraper will house two structures earmarked for residential spaces and built on top of two large commercial floors. An eye-catching undulating stone and glass protection layer envelops the building, providing visual continuity. The complex will have a number of attractive features that are fairly unusual in Manhattan, such as a small pine forest in the garden and a labyrinth of hedges on the roof between the two residential towers.

Ce gratte-ciel à usage mixte abritera deux structures destinées à des espaces résidentiels, érigées sur deux grands étages à usage commercial. Une cuirasse ondulante spectaculaire en pierre et en verre enveloppe le volume et lui apporte sa continuité visuelle. Le complexe est doté d'attraits peu courants à Manhattan, comme son petit bois de pins dans le jardin et un labyrinthe de haies sur le toit entre les deux tours résidentielles.

Questo grattacielo d'uso misto ospiterà due strutture per spazi residenziali, edificate sue due grandi piani d'uso commerciale. Una vistosa corazza ondulata di pietra e cristallo avvolge il fabbricato, conferendogli una continuità visiva. Il complesso possiede elementi accattivanti, che non sono molto comuni a Manhattan, quali un piccolo bosco di pini nel giardino e un labirinto di siepi sul tetto, tra le due torri residenziali.

Dieser multifunktionale Wolkenkratzer wird nach Fertigstellung zwei Baukörper umfassen, die für Wohnungen reserviert sind und auf zwei großen Etagen mit gewerblicher Nutzung errichtet sind. Eine auffällig gewellte Schutzhülle umgibt den Baukörper und verleiht ihm visuelle Homogenität. Der Baukomplex hat Reize, die in Manhattan eher unüblich sind, nämlich einen kleinen Pinienwald im Garten und ein Heckenlabyrinth auf dem Dach zwischen den beiden Wohntürmen.

Deze multifunctionele wolkenkrabber voor gemengd gebruik zal twee structuren omvatten die bestemd zijn voor residentiële ruimten bovenop twee commerciële etages. Een opvallende schild uit steen en glas omhult het volume waardoor visuele continuïteit gewaarborgd wordt. Het complex biedt enkele kenmerken die in Manhattan niet echt gebruikelijk zijn, zoals een klein dennenbos in de tuin en een haaglabyrint op het dak, tussen de twee woontorens.

Este rascacielos de uso mixto albergará dos estructuras destinadas a espacios residenciales, erigidas sobre dos grandes plantas de uso comercial. Una llamativa coraza ondulante de piedra y cristal envuelve el volumen, aportándole continuidad visual. El complejo cuenta con atractivos no demasiado comunes en Manhattan, como son un pequeño bosque de pinos en el jardín y un laberinto de setos en la cubierta, entre las dos torres residenciales.

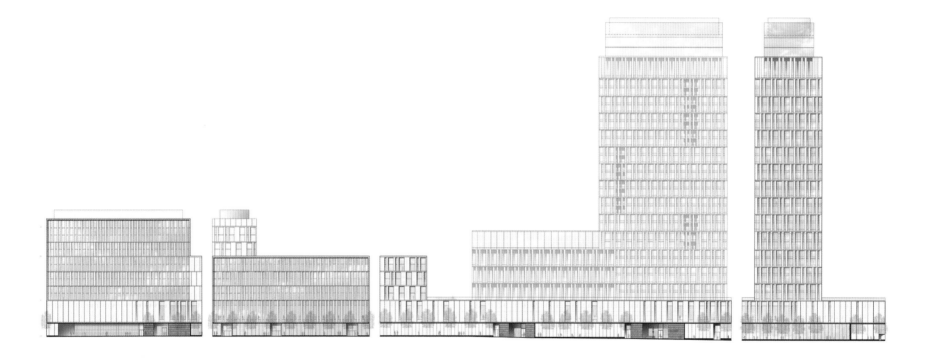

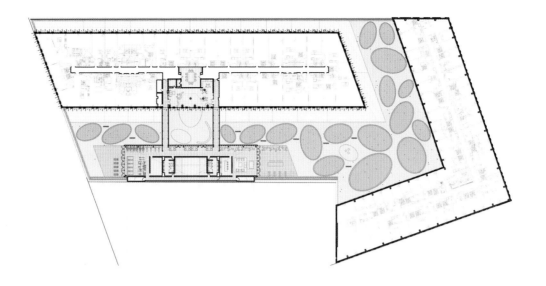

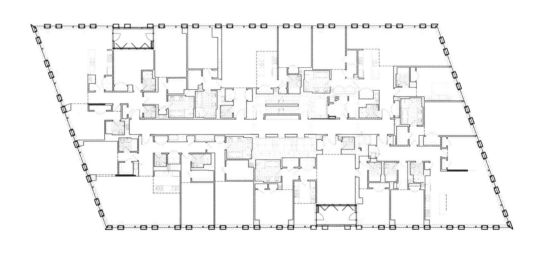

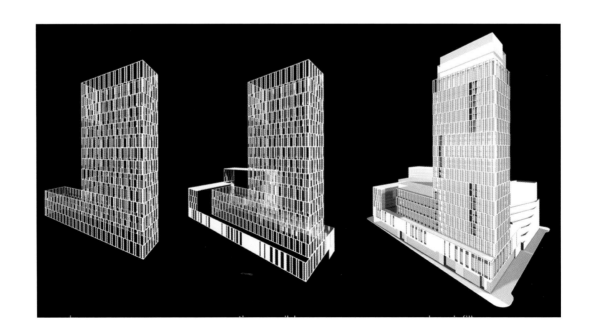

SMITH-MILLER & HAWKINSON ARCHITECTS

Greenberg Loft

The brief for remodeling this home was to provide living space and a place to exhibit art works. The client, an art collector, wanted these two functions to coexist without strict boundaries between daily life and love of art. In order to cater to this requirement, the architects came up with cross designs that allowed the art gallery to blend into the private spaces.

C'est avec pour consigne que l'appartement puisse à la fois servir de logement et de galerie d'exposition que la rénovation a été effectuée. Le client, collectionneur d'art, souhaitait que ces deux fonctions cohabitent, sans frontière stricte entre son quotidien, sa vie et sa passion pour l'art. Pour cela, les architectes ont mis au point des plans croisés dans lesquels galerie et parties privées se confondent.

Questa struttura è stata rinnovata con l'obiettivo di creare un'abitazione e uno spazio espositivo in cui ospitare delle opere d'arte. Il cliente, un collezionista, desiderava che queste due funzioni si integrassero senza creare una rigorosa delimitazione tra la vita di ogni giorno e il suo amore per l'arte. A tal fine gli architetti hanno sviluppato dei programmi incrociati in cui la galleria si unisce alle zone private.

Diese Wohnung wurde nach der Vorgabe reformiert, eine Wohnung und einen Ausstellungsbereich für Kunstwerke aufzunehmen. Der Auftraggeber, ein Kunstsammler, wollte, dass beide Funktionen ohne strenge Grenzen zwischen seinem täglichen Ablauf und Leben, wie auch seiner Neigung für die Kunst zusammenleben. Zu diesem Zweck entwarfen die Architekten gekreuzte Programme, bei denen die Galerie in die Privatbereiche übergeht.

De opdracht voor de verbouwing van deze woning was een ruimte creëren die zowel de woning als een tentoonstellingsruimte voor kunstwerken moest herbergen. De klant, een kunstverzamelaar, wenste dat deze twee functies zouden samenleven zonder dat zijn dagelijkse ontwikkeling, zijn leven of zijn passie voor kunst daardoor strikt afgebakend werden. Daarvoor ontwikkelden de architecten gekruiste programma's waarin de galerij met de privézones samensmelt.

El objetivo del proyecto de reforma de esta residencia era proporcionar espacios donde vivir y donde exponer obras de arte. El cliente, un coleccionista de arte, quería que estas dos funciones convivieran sin existir fronteras estrictas entre su su vida diaria y su afición al arte. Para ello, los arquitectos desarrollaron programas cruzados en los que la galería se confunde con las zonas privadas.

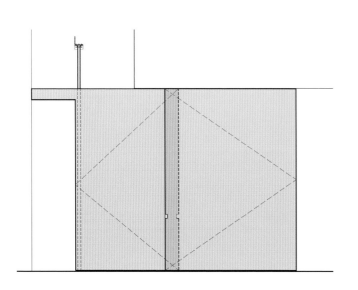
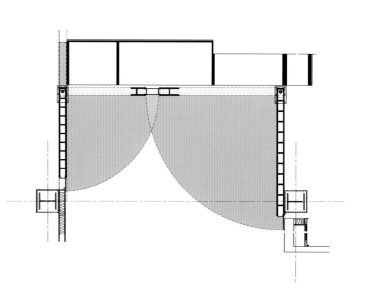

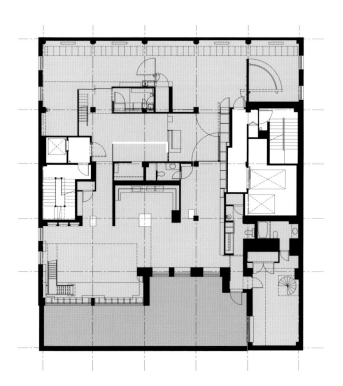
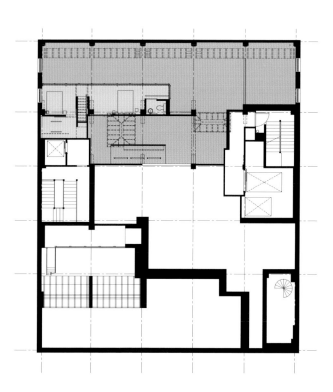

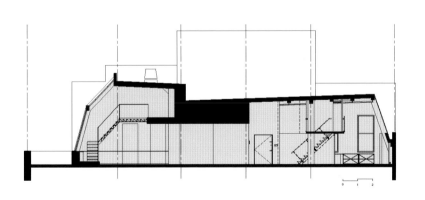
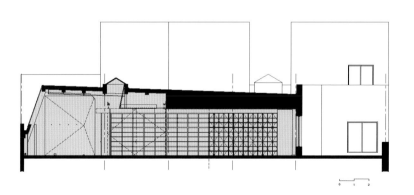

NYU Department of Philosophy

Following the remodeling work done, the new NYU Department of Philosophy features offices, seminar rooms, a library, vestibule and an auditorium for 120 people. The principal premise of the new configuration is to make better use of natural light. One example is the design of the staircase. The permeable structure permits light to pass through from the new skylight above, with impressive results.

Après leur rénovation, les nouveaux locaux du département de philosophie de cette université new-yorkaise hébergent des bureaux, des salles de séminaire, une bibliothèque, un vestibule et un auditorium de 120 places. La nouvelle configuration des lieux s'attache avant tout à tirer un meilleur parti de la lumière naturelle. Les escaliers sont un bon exemple de cette volonté. Leur structure poreuse laisse passer la lumière qui vient de la lucarne qui les surplombe, avec un résultat spectaculaire.

In seguito alla ristrutturazione, le nuove ali del dipartimento di filosofia di questa università newyorchese ospitano uffici, studi di seminario, una biblioteca, un vestibolo e un auditorium con una capienza di 120 posti. La premessa principale della nuova configurazione è un migliore sfruttamento della luce naturale. Un esempio di ciò è costituito dal design delle scale: la loro struttura porosa permette il passaggio della luce dal nuovo lucernario superiore, con incredibili risultati.

Nach dem Umbau beherbergen die neuen Zweigstellen der philosophischen Fakultät der New York University Büros, Seminarräume, eine Bibliothek, eine Vorhalle und ein Auditorium, das für 120 Hörer angelegt ist. Hauptprämisse der neuen Anlage war, das Tageslicht besser auszunutzen. Ein Beispiel für die Umsetzung dieser Parole ist die Gestaltung des Treppenhauses. Seine durchlässige Struktur erlaubt, dass das Licht, von dem neuen Oberlicht ausgehend, bis nach unten dringt. Die Wirkung ist beeindruckend.

Na de verbouwing herbergen de nieuwe ruimten van het filosofiedepartement van deze New Yorkse universiteit kantoren, seminarieruimten, een bibliotheek, een foyer en een auditorium met een capaciteit voor 120 toehoorders. De nieuwe configuratie hanteert als belangrijkste premisse het natuurlijk licht beter benutten. Een voorbeeld hiervan is het ontwerp van de trap. De poreuze structuur laat vanaf het nieuwe dakvenster het licht door en zorgt voor indrukwekkende resultaten.

Tras la remodelación llevada a cabo, las nuevas dependencias del departamento de filosofía de esta universidad neoyorquina albergan oficinas, despachos de seminario, una biblioteca, un vestíbulo y un auditorio con capacidad para 120 asistentes. La nueva configuración maneja como principal premisa un mejor aprovechamiento de la luz natural. Un ejemplo de esta consigna es el diseño de las escaleras. Su estructura porosa deja pasar la luz que entra a través de la nueva claraboya superior, con impresionantes resultados.

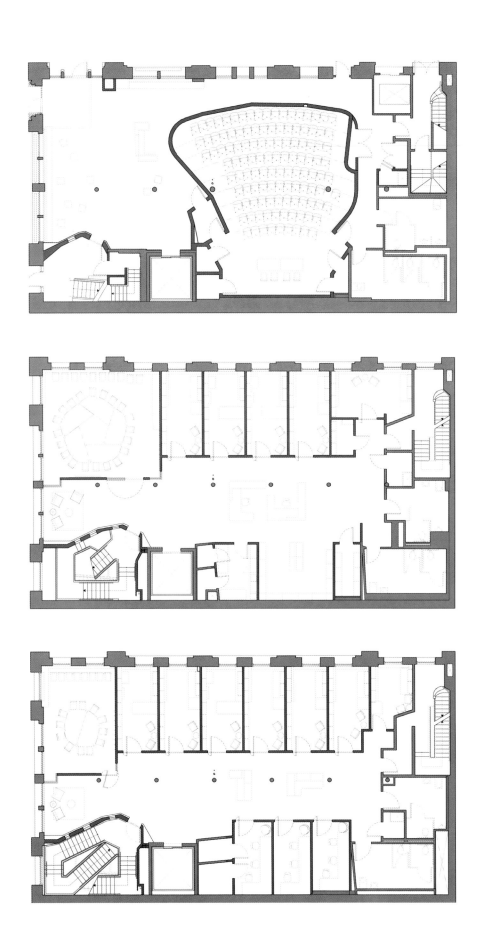

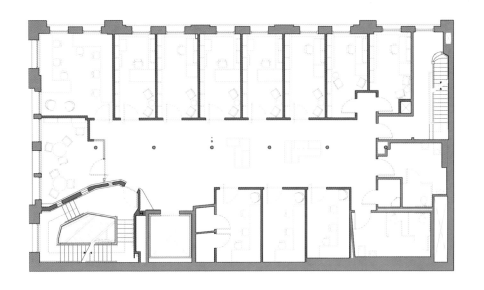

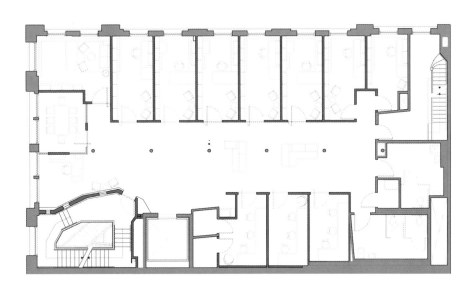

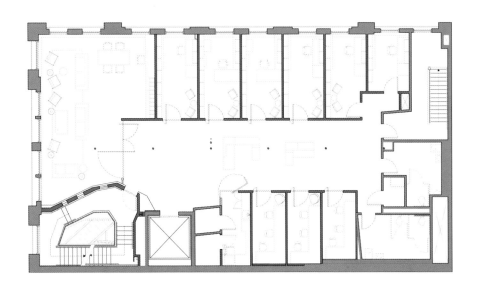

STONELY PELSINSKI ARCHITECTS NEUKOMM

GoSmile Aesthetics

Poor circulation between spaces and the complicated vestibule were the big challenges for the designers when it came to renovating this dental clinic. Drawing on the GoSmile packaging as the inspiration, the receptionist's desk has been designed to look like it has doubled. Similarly, the enameled sheen of healthy teeth is evoked in the finishes of most of the areas in the space, which appear to be lined in porcelain.

La mauvaise circulation entre les espaces et la configuration alambiquée du vestibule ont considérablement compliqué la tâche des décorateurs chargés de l'aménagement de cette clinique dentaire. Le comptoir de réception est inspiré de la façon dont GoSmile emballe ses produits, et donne l'impression de se dédoubler. Dans le même esprit, la finition de la plupart des surfaces de l'espace, qui semblent recouvertes de porcelaine, évoque l'émail des dents en bonne santé.

La cattiva circolazione tra gli ambienti e il carattere intricato del vestibolo hanno costituito una grossa sfida per i progettisti nella preparazione di questa clinica dentale. Ispirandosi al modo in cui la marca GoSmile impacchetta i suoi prodotti, il design della console della reception crea un effetto ottico per cui quest'ultima sembra sdoppiarsi. In un modo simile, l'aspetto smaltato dei denti sani è evocato mediante le rifiniture della maggior parte delle superfici dello spazio, che sembrano ricoperte di porcellana.

Die schlechte Erschließung der Räume und der unübersichtlichen Vorhalle stellten eine große Herausforderung für die Innenarchitekten dieser Zahnklinik dar. Man ließ sich von der Art und Weise anregen, wie die Marke GoSmile ihre Produkte verpackt, und erreichte dadurch, dass die Sockelgestaltung der Rezeption den Eindruck vermittelt, als würde sie sich aufbiegen. Auf ähnliche Weise wecken die meisten Oberflächen im Raum die Assoziation an den emaillefarbenen Anblick gesunder Zähne; sie wirken wie mit Porzellan verkleidet.

Moeilijke circulatie tussen de verschillende ruimten en een gecompliceerde hal vormden de grote uitdaging voor de ontwerpers die deze tandkliniek moesten renoveren. Voor het ontwerp van de receptiebalie lieten ze zich inspireren door de verpakkingen van de GoSmile producten en dit resulteerde in een dubbel gevouwen indruk. Op gelijkaardige wijze doen de met porselein afgewerkte oppervlakken denken aan het emailwit van gezonde tanden.

La mala circulación entre espacios y lo intrincado del vestíbulo supusieron un gran reto para los arquitectos a la hora de acondicionar esta clínica dental. Inspirándose en la manera en que la marca GoSmile empaqueta sus productos, diseñaron una consola de recepción que parece desdoblarse. Asimismo, el aspecto esmaltado de unos dientes sanos se evoca con los acabados de la mayor parte de las superficies del espacio, que parecen forradas de porcelana.

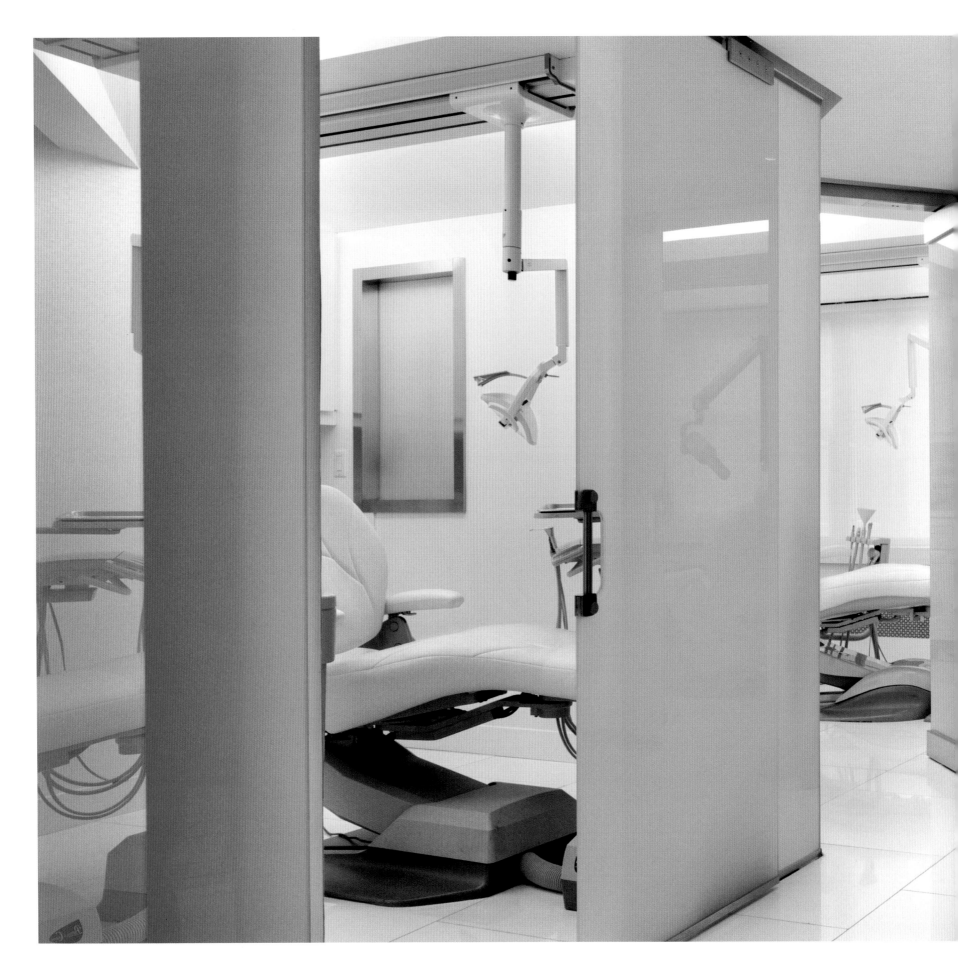

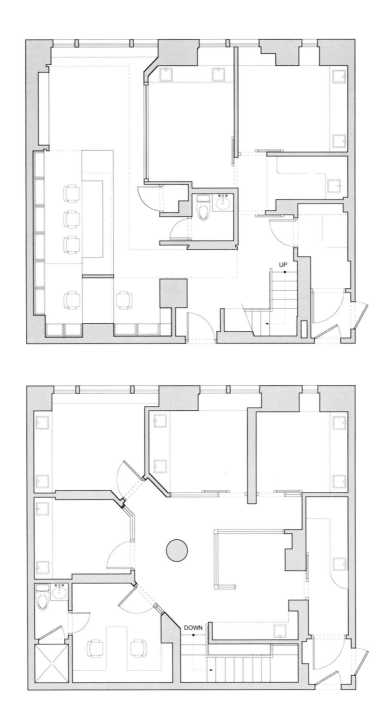

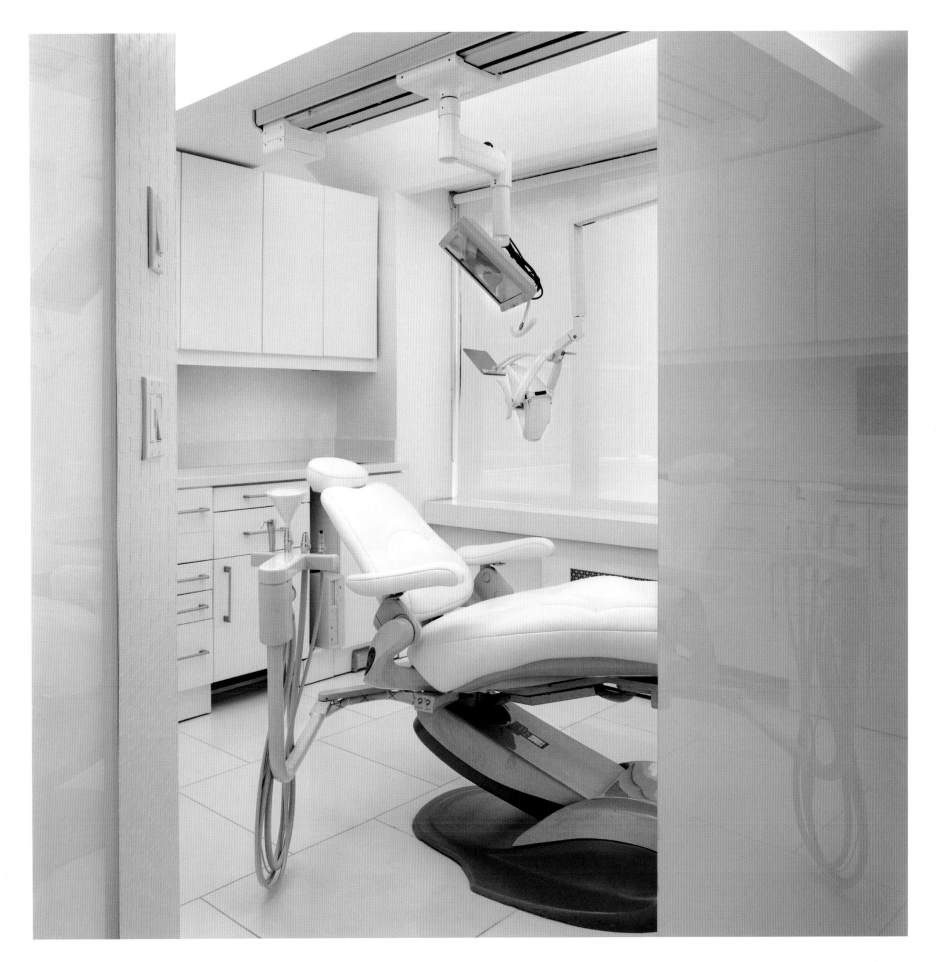

STONELY PELSINSKI ARCHITECTS NEUKOMM

Sullens Residence

The owners' predilection for Frank Lloyd Wright architecture had a big impact on the spirit of the interior design of this home and explains the wood coverings and classic Venetian shutters and blinds. The configuration of this duplex, previously used as a photography studio, enabled the addition of two mezzanines and the rehabilitation of a central atrium to connect them. The absence of exterior spaces motivated the creation of a solarium at the southern end to prevent any feeling of claustrophobia and to adapt a space for a garden.

Les propriétaires ont une prédilection pour l'architecture de Frank Lloyd Wright, et cela se retrouve beaucoup dans l'esprit de la décoration de cette résidence. C'est de là que vient l'abondance de revêtements en bois et de persiennes et stores classiques. La configuration de ce duplex, un ancien studio de photographie, a permis d'ajouter deux mezzanines et d'aménager une galerie qui les relie. Pour pallier l'absence d'espaces extérieurs, on a créé un solarium à l'extrémité sud. Il évite toute sensation de claustrophobie et donne un espace propice au jardinage.

La predilezione dei proprietari per l'architettura di Frank Lloyd Wright ha caratterizzato in gran misura lo spirito del design d'interni di questa residenza; da tale concetto deriva il predominio di rivestimenti di legno e di persiane e tendine classiche. La configurazione di questo duplex, in precedenza utilizzato come studio di fotografia, ha permesso di aggiungere due soppalchi e di abilitare un atrio centrale per metterli in comunicazione. L'assenza di spazi esterni ha prodotto la creazione di un solarium nell'estremità sud, per evitare una possibile sensazione di claustrofobia e allestire uno spazio propizio al giardinaggio.

Die ausgesprochene Vorliebe der Eigentümer für die Architektur von Frank Lloyd Wright prägte weitgehend den Geist der Innengestaltung dieser Residenz; daher herrschen auch Holzverkleidungen sowie klassische Jalousien und Fensterläden vor. Die Anlage dieser Maisonettewohnung, die zuvor als Fotostudio diente, erlaubte es, zwei Zwischengeschosse einzubauen und das zentrale Atrium als Verbindungsglied dazwischen anzupassen. Weil Außenbereiche fehlen, schuf man an der Südseite einen Erker, um klaustrophobische Gefühle zu vermeiden und die Bedingungen für einen Ort zu schaffen, der sich als Garten eignet.

De voorliefde van de eigenaars voor de architectuur van Frank Lloyd Wright kenmerkte grotendeels de interieursfeer van dit woningontwerp; vandaar de overheersende houten wandbekledingen en de klassieke luiken en stores. De configuratie van deze duplex, een voormalige fotografiestudio, maakte het mogelijk twee mezzanines en een centraal atrium toe te voegen om ze onderling te verbinden. De afwezigheid van buitenruimten gaf aanleiding tot de creatie van een solarium aan de zuidkant om een mogelijk gevoel van claustrofobie te vermijden en een ruimte te creëren die als tuin dienst kan doen.

La predilección de los propietarios por la arquitectura de Frank Lloyd Wright marcó en gran medida el espíritu del diseño de interiores de esta residencia: de ahí el predominio de recubrimientos en madera y de persianas y estores clásicos. La configuración de este dúplex, anteriormente utilizado como estudio de fotografía, permitió añadir dos altillos y habilitar un atrio central para conectarlos. La ausencia de espacios exteriores motivó la creación de un solárium en el extremo sur, para evitar una posible sensación de claustrofobia y acondicionar un espacio propicio para la jardinería.

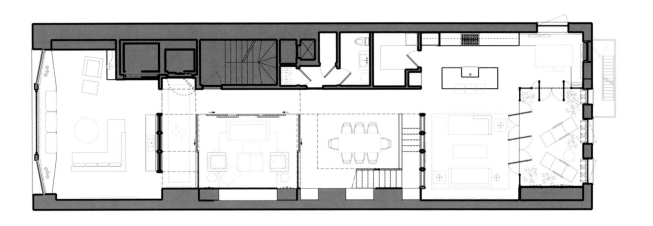

THE APARTMENT CREATIVE AGENCY

The Black Apartment

The owner's desire to feel like being "in a bar in Shanghai at nightfall" led to a design in the form of an apartment with totally black walls, ceilings, and floors, with no divisions excepte for the two bathrooms. The owner saw the choice of color as an excellent opportunity to display her eclectic collection of furniture, art, and books, including her passion for designer shoes.

Afin de respecter le désir de la propriétaire de se sentir « dans un bar de Shanghai à la tombée de la nuit », la proposition a revêtu la forme d'un appartement aux murs, plafond et plancher entièrement noirs, dépourvu de cloisons de séparation, hormis pour les deux salles de bain. La propriétaire a vu dans ce choix de couleur une excellente opportunité pour exposer sa collection de meubles, d'art et de livres éclectique ainsi que sa passion pour les chaussures signées par des créateurs.

Seguendo il desiderio della proprietaria di sentirsi «in un bar di Shanghai all'imbrunire», la proposta è stata quella di realizzare un appartamento con pareti, soffitti e pavimenti completamente neri, senza pareti divisorie a eccezione dei due bagni. La proprietaria ha visto nella scelta di questo colore un'ottima opportunità per dare risalto alla propria eclettica collezione di mobili, oggetti artistici e libri, tra cui figura la sua passione per le scarpe firmate da famosi stilisti.

Nach Wunsch der Eigentümerin, sich wie "in einer Bar in Schanghai am Abend" zu fühlen, entstand der Vorschlag eines Appartements mit komplett schwarzen Wänden, Decken und Böden ohne Trennwände - ausgenommen in den beiden Bädern. Die Eigentümerin sah in der Farbwahl eine ausgezeichnete Gelegenheit, ihre eklektische Möbel-, Kunst- und Buchsammlung, wie auch ihre Vorliebe für von Designern signierte Schuhe, zur Schau zu stellen.

De wens van de eigenares om zich "in een bar van nachtelijk Sjanghai" te wanen, zorgde ervoor dat het voorstel bestond uit een appartement met volledig zwarte vloeren en plafonds, zonder tussenwanden, met uitzondering van de twee badkamers. De eigenares zag in de kleurkeuze een uitstekende gelegenheid om haar eclectische verzameling meubels, kunst en boeken ten toon te stellen, inclusief haar passie voor designschoenen van beroemde ontwerpers.

El deseo de la propietaria de sentirse como «en un bar de Shanghai al caer la noche» se concretó en un apartamento de paredes, techos y suelo completamente negros, sin paredes divisorias, excepto en los dos baños. La propietaria vio en la elección del color una excelente oportunidad para exhibir su ecléctica colección de muebles, arte y libros, incluso su pasión por los zapatos firmados por diseñadores.

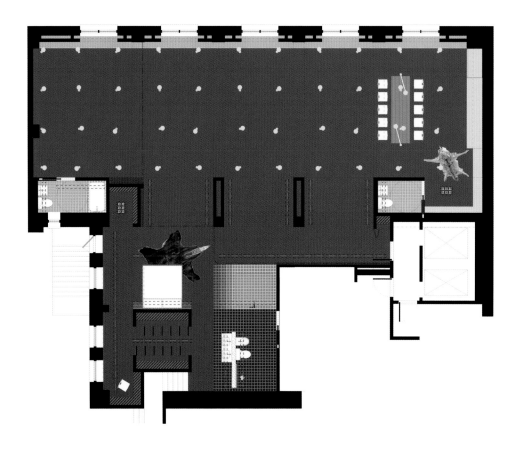

TOBA + PAIK ARCHITECTS

Martins Loft

Two apartments were remodeled to create a single, open-plan space. This loft serves as a residence and place of work. The lower level was restructured to create a generous white space that was free of distractions. A metal staircase connects both levels. Multifunctional furniture was chosen to cover the requirements of both uses and for the purpose of maximizing space.

Deux appartements ont été réaménagés afin de créer une pièce unique et ouverte. Ce loft fait office de logement ainsi que de lieu de travail. Le rez-de-chaussée a été rénové de manière à créer une pièce spacieuse et de couleur blanche, sans fioritures. Un escalier en métal relie les deux appartements. Du mobilier à caractère multifonctionnel a été privilégié afin de répondre à la nécessité d'ambivalence des lieux et d'optimiser l'espace.

Questo ambiente unico e aperto è il risultato della ristrutturazione di due appartamenti. Il *loft* ha la funzione di abitazione e luogo di lavoro allo stesso tempo. La parte inferiore è stata rinnovata per creare un ambiente spazioso, bianco e libero da distrazioni. Una scala in metallo collega i due appartamenti. I mobili scelti sono multifunzione e soddisfano le necessità del doppio uso dell'ambiente ottimizzando così gli spazi a disposizione.

Zwei Wohnungen wurden umgebaut, um einen einheitlichen offenen Bereich zu schaffen. Dieses *Loft* dient als Wohnung und Arbeitsstätte. Der untere Teil wurde umgebaut, um ein geräumiges und weißes Ambiente frei von Ablenkungen zu schaffen. Eine Metalltreppe verbindet beide Etagen. Die Möbel wurden als Mehrzweckmöbel gewählt, um den Bedarf beiden Nutzungen in Wohnung abzudecken und den Platz zu optimieren.

Twee flats werden verbouwd om één enkele, open ruimte te creëren. Deze *loft* doet dienst als woning en werkplaats. Het onderste deel werd verbouwd om een ruime en witte ruimte te creëren, vrij van afleidingen. Een metalen trap verbindt beide flats. Het meubilair werd gekozen vanwege de multifunctionaliteit om aan de dubbele gebruiksbehoeften van de plaats te voldoen en de ruimte te optimaliseren.

Este *loft*, resultado de la reforma de dos pisos para crear un único ambiente, funciona como vivienda y como lugar de trabajo. La parte inferior se remodeló para crear un espacioso y blanco ambiente libre de distracciones. Una escalera de metal conecta ambos pisos. Se eligió un mobiliario multifuncional para cubrir las necesidades de los dos usos del lugar y con la intención de optimizar el espacio.

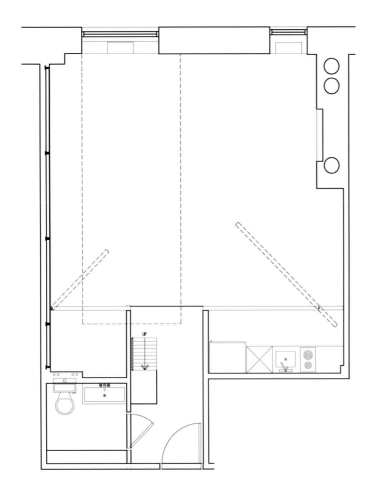
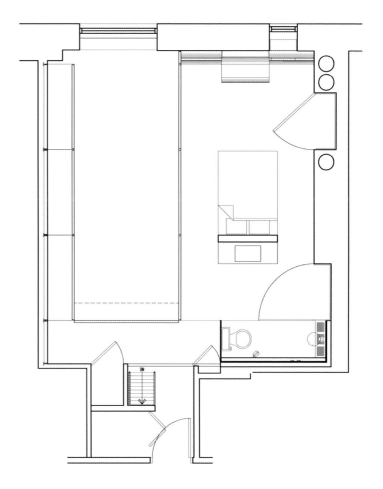

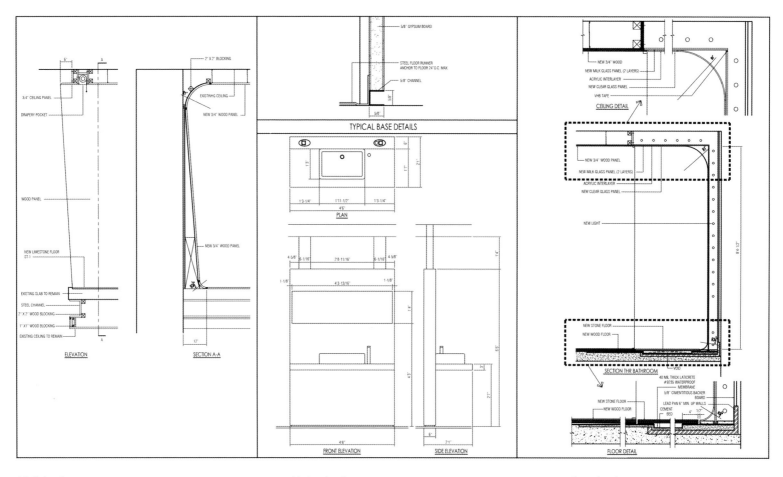

Wall details

Vanity details

Glass details

DIRECTORY

Agence Christophe Pillet
29 passage Dubail, 75010 Paris, France
P +33 158 364 631
www.christophepillet.com
info@christophepillet.com
Catherine Malandrino Boutique
Photos © Cati Gonzales, Barbel Miebach

Alden Maddry
218 St John's Place, Apt 3F, Brooklyn, New York, NY 11217, USA
P +1 917 204 9119
www.aldenmaddry.com
Phillips-Skaife Residence
Photos © Jordi Miralles
Park West Apartment
Photos © Matteo Piazza

Ali Tayar
416 West 13th Street, Suite 316 C, New York, NY 10014, USA
P +1 212 989 4959
www.alitayar.com
mtayar@rcn.com
Pizza Bar
Pop Burger
Photos © Joshua McHugh

Allen + Killcoyne Architects
12 West 27th Street, 17th Floor, New York, NY 10001, USA
P +1 212 645 2222
www.allen-killcoyne.com
tliebl@allen-killcoyne.com
Redken 3
Photos © Michael Weber
Tenant Amenities
Photos © Taylor Photo

Allied Works Architecture
12 West 27th Street, 18th Floor, New York, NY 10001, USA
P +1 212 431 9476
www.alliedworks.com
info@alliedworks.com
Museum of Arts and Design

Archi-Tectonics
11 Hubert Street, New York, NY 10013, USA
P +1 212 226 0303
www.archi-tectonics.com
office@archi-tectonics.com
V33 Residential Building

ArchLab
One Union Square West 506, New York, NY 10003, USA
P +1 212 647 1399
www.archlabstudio.com
antonio@archlabstudio.com
Tibi Boutique
Photos © Adrian Wilson

Arthur Casas Arquitetura e Design
Rua Itápolis 818, São Paulo
SP 01245 000, Brazil
P +55 11 2182 7500
www.arthurcasas.com
sp@arthurcasas.com
Penthouse in Chelsea
Photos © Tuca Reinés

Bonetti/Kozerski Studio
270 Lafayette Street, Suite 906, New York, NY 10012, USA
P +1 212 343 9898
www.bonettikozerski.com
info@bonettikozerski.com
Duplex Apartment
Park West Apartment
Photos © Matteo Piazza

CCS Architecture
180 Varick Street 902, New York, NY 10014, USA
P +1 212 274 1121
www.ccs-architecture.com
Greenwhich Village Condominium
Photos © Javier Haddad Conde

Desai/Chia Architecture
54 West 21st Street, 7th Floor, New York, NY 10010, USA
P +1 212 366 9630
www.desaichia.com
info@desaichia.com
Loft in Cooper Square
Renovated Loft
Photos © Paul Warchol

Elmslie Osler
526 West 26th Street, Suite 514, New York, NY 10001, USA
P +1 212 989 0652
www.eoarch.com
mail@eoarch.com
Amaridian
Photos © Frank Oudeman

Ghislaine Viñas Interior Design
67 Vestry Street, 8b, New York, NY 10013, USA
P +1 212 219 7678
www.gvinteriors.com
info@gvinteriors.som
Chelsea Gallery
Photos © Michael Moran

Hariri & Hariri Architecture
39 West 29th Street, 12th Floor, New York, NY 10001, USA
P +1 212 727 0338
www.haririandhariri.com
info@haririandhariri.com
Juan Valdez Flagship Café
Page Residence
Photos © Paul Warchol

James Slade/Slade Architecture
150 Broadway 807, New York, NY 10038, USA
P +1 212 677 6380
www.sladearch.com
Flatiron Loft
Hochhauser Residence
Noho Loft
Photos © Jordi Miralles

John Barman
500 Park Avenue, New York, NY 10022, USA
P +1 212 839 9443
www.johnbarman.com
John Barman Residence
Photos © Billy Cunningham

John Lee, Alex Gil, Karin Tehve/Workshop for Architecture
526 West 26th Street, Suite 410, New York, NY 10001, USA
P +1 212 674 3400
www.wfora.com
Swinehart Loft
Photos © Floto+Warner

Jordan Mozer & Associates
320 West Ohio, 7th Floor, Chicago, IL 60610, USA
P +1 312 397 1133
www.mozer.com
invention@mozer.com
Renaissance Hotel
Photos © Jeff Zaruba

Karim Rashid

357 West 17th St., New York, NY 10011, USA

P +1 212 929 8657

www.karimrashid.com

Loft by Karim Rashid

Photos © Jean François Jussaud

Kazuyo Sejima & Ryue Nishizawa/SANAA

7-A Shinagawa-Soko, 2-2-35 Higashi-Shinagawa, 140 Tokyo, Japan

P +81 3 3450 1754

www.sanaa.co.jp

sanaa@sanaa.co.jp

New Museum of Contemporary Art

Photos © Dean Kaufman

Lewis.Tsurumaki.Lewis/LTL Architects

227 West 29th Street, 7th Floor, New York, NY 10001, USA

P +1 212 505 5955

www.ltlarchitects.com

office@ltlarchitects.com

Geltner Parker Loft

© Lewis.Tsurumaki.Lewis

Xing Restaurant

Photos © Michael Moran

Michael Overington & Anda Andrei/Ian Schrager Company

818 Greenwich Street, New York, NY 10014, USA

P +1 212 796 8400

www.ianschragercompany.com

info@ianschragercompany.com

Gramercy Park Hotel

Photos © Ian Schrager Company

nArchitects

68 Jay Street, 317, Brooklyn, NY 11201, USA

P +1 718 260 0845

www.narchitects.com

n@narchitects.com

Switch Building

Photos © Frank Oudeman

Renzo Piano Building Workshop

Via Rubens 29, 16158 Genova, Italy

P +39 010 61 711

www.rpbw.com

italy@rpbw.com

The New York Times Building

Photos © Michel Denancé

Resolution: 4 Architecture

150 West 28th Street, Suite 1902, New York, NY 10001, USA

P +1 212 675 9266

www.re4a.com

Eisenman Davidson

© Jeff Goldberg, Esto

Nychay Loft

Photos © Floto+Warner

Rios Clementi Hale Studios

639 N Larchmont Blvd, Los Angeles, CA 90004, USA

P +1 323 785 1800

www.rchstudios.com

frank@rchstudios.com

Coulter Apartment

Photos © Michael Moran

Skidmore, Owings & Merrill LLP

14 Wall Street, 24th Floor, New York, NY 10005, USA

P +1 212 298 9300

www.som.com

somnewyork@som.com

7 World Trade Center

Photos © Chuck Choi, Eric Laignel, Ruggero Vani

Tribeca Building

Smith-Miller & Hawkinson Architects LLP

305 Canal Street, New York, NY 10013, USA

P +1 212 966 3875

www.smharch.com

Greenberg Loft

Photos © Matteo Piazza

Steven Holl Architects

450 West 31st Street, 11th Floor, New York, NY 10001, USA

P +1 212 629 7262

www.stevenholl.com

newyork@stevenholl.com

NYU Department of Philosophy

Photos © Andy Ryan

Stonely Pelsinski Architects Neukomm LLC

11 Broadway, Suite 1500, New York, NY 10004, USA

P +1 212 732 7012

www.span-ny.com

partners@span-ny.com

GoSmile Aesthetics

Sullens Residence

Photos © Michael Moran

The Apartment Creative Agency

101 Crosby St., New York, NY 10012, USA

P +1 212 219 3661

www.theapt.com

The Black Apartment

Photos © Michael Weber

Toba + Paik Architects

304 Hudson Street, 6th Floor, New York, NY 10013, USA

P +1 212 431 1088

www.paikholtzer.com

Martins Loft

Photos © Hothousestudios.net